CERTAIN PERSONAL MATTERS

H. G. WELLS

1st WORLD
LIBRARY
Literary Society

Certain Personal Matters

H. G. Wells

© 1st World Library, 2006
PO Box 2211
Fairfield, IA 52556
www.1stworldlibrary.com
First Edition

LCCN: 2007920648

Softcover ISBN: 978-1-4218-3959-2
Hardcover ISBN: 978-1-4218-3859-5
eBook ISBN: 978-1-4218-4059-8

Purchase *"Certain Personal Matters"*
as a traditional bound book at:
www.1stWorldLibrary.com/purchase.asp?ISBN=978-1-4218-3959-2

1st World Library is a literary, educational organization
dedicated to:

- Creating a free internet library of downloadable ebooks

- Hosting writing competitions and offering book
publishing scholarships.

1ˢᵗ World Library Literary Society

Giving Back to the World

"If you want to work on the core problem, it's early school literacy."

- James Barksdale, former CEO of Netscape

"No skill is more crucial to the future of a child, or to a democratic and prosperous society, than literacy."

- Los Angeles Times

Literacy... means far more than learning how to read and write... The aim is to transmit... knowledge and promote social participation."

- UNESCO

"Literacy is not a luxury, it is a right and a responsibility. If our world is to meet the challenges of the twenty-first century we must harness the energy and creativity of all our citizens."

- President Bill Clinton

"Parents should be encouraged to read to their children, and teachers should be equipped with all available techniques for teaching literacy, so the varying needs and capacities of individual kids can be taken into account."

- Hugh Mackay

CONTENTS

THOUGHTS ON CHEAPNESS
AND MY AUNT CHARLOTTE

The world mends. In my younger days people believed in mahogany; some of my readers will remember it—a heavy, shining substance, having a singularly close resemblance to raw liver, exceedingly heavy to move, and esteemed on one or other count the noblest of all woods. Such of us as were very poor and had no mahogany pretended to have mahogany; and the proper hepatite tint was got by veneering. That makes one incline to think it was the colour that pleased people. In those days there was a word "trashy," now almost lost to the world. My dear Aunt Charlotte used that epithet when, in her feminine way, she swore at people she did not like. "Trashy" and "paltry" and "Brummagem" was the very worst she could say of them. And she had, I remember, an intense aversion to plated goods and bronze halfpence. The halfpence of her youth had been vast and corpulent red-brown discs, which it was folly to speak of as small change. They were fine handsome coins, and almost as inconvenient as crown-pieces. I remember she corrected me once when I was very young. "Don't call a penny a copper, dear," she said; "copper is a metal. The pennies they have nowadays are bronze." It is odd how our childish impressions cling to us. I still regard bronze as a kind of upstart intruder, a mere trashy pretender among metals.

All my Aunt Charlotte's furniture was thoroughly good, and most of it extremely uncomfortable; there was not a thing for a little boy to break and escape damnation in the household. Her china was the only thing with a touch of beauty in it—at least I remember nothing else—and each of her blessed plates was worth the happiness of a mortal for days together. And they dressed me in a Nessus suit of valuable garments. I learned the value of thoroughly good things only too early. I knew the equivalent of a teacup to the very last scowl, and I have hated good, handsome property ever since. For my part I love cheap things, trashy things, things made of the commonest rubbish that money can possibly buy; things as vulgar as primroses, and as transitory as a morning's frost.

Think of all the advantages of a cheap possession—cheap and nasty, if you will—compared with some valuable substitute. Suppose you need this or that. "Get a good one," advises Aunt Charlotte; "one that will last." You do—and it does last. It lasts like a family curse. These great plain valuable things, as plain as good women, as complacently assured of their intrinsic worth—who does not know them? My Aunt Charlotte scarcely had a new thing in her life. Her mahogany was avuncular; her china remotely ancestral; her feather beds and her bedsteads!—they were haunted; the births, marriages, and deaths associated with the best one was the history of our race for three generations. There was more in her house than the tombstone rectitude of the chair-backs to remind me of the graveyard. I can still remember the sombre aisles of that house, the vault-like shadows, the magnificent window curtains that blotted out the windows. Life was too trivial for such things. She never knew she tired of them, but she did. That was the secret of her temper, I think; they engendered her sombre Calvinism, her perception of the trashy quality of human life. The pretence that they were the accessories to human life was too transparent. *We* were the accessories; we minded them for a little while, and then we passed away. They wore us out and cast us aside. We were the changing scenery; they were the actors who played on through the piece. It was even so with clothing. We buried my other maternal aunt—Aunt Adelaide—and wept, and partly forgot her; but her wonderful silk dresses—they would stand alone—still went rustling cheerfully about an ephemeral world.

H. G. Wells

All that offended my sense of proportion, my feeling of what is due to human life, even when I was a little boy. I want things of my own, things I can break without breaking my heart; and, since one can live but once, I want some change in my life—to have this kind of thing and then that. I never valued Aunt Charlotte's good old things until I sold them. They sold remarkably well: those chairs like nether millstones for the grinding away of men; the fragile china—an incessant anxiety until accident broke it, and the spell of it at the same time; those silver spoons, by virtue of which Aunt Charlotte went in fear of burglary for six-and-fifty years; the bed from which I alone of all my kindred had escaped; the wonderful old, erect, high-shouldered, silver-faced clock.

But, as I say, our ideas are changing—mahogany has gone, and repp curtains. Articles are made for man, nowadays, and not man, by careful early training, for articles. I feel myself to be in many respects a link with the past. Commodities come like the spring flowers, and vanish again. "Who steals my watch steals trash," as some poet has remarked; the thing is made of I know not what metal, and if I leave it on the mantel for a day or so it goes a deep blackish purple that delights me exceedingly. My grandfather's hat—I understood when I was a little boy that I was to have that some day. But now I get a hat for ten shillings, or less, two or three times a year. In the old days buying clothes was well-nigh as irrevocable as marriage. Our flat is furnished with glittering things—wanton arm-chairs just strong enough not to collapse under you, books in gay covers, carpets you are free to drop lighted fusees upon; you may scratch what you like, upset your coffee, cast your cigar ash to the four quarters of heaven. Our guests, at anyrate, are not snubbed by our furniture. It knows its place.

But it is in the case of art and adornment that cheapness is most delightful. The only thing that betrayed a care for beauty on the part of my aunt was her dear old flower garden, and even there she was not above suspicion. Her favourite flowers were tulips, rigid tulips with opulent crimson streaks. She despised wildings. Her ornaments were simply displays of the precious metal. Had she known the price of platinum she would have worn that by preference. Her chains and brooches and rings were bought by weight. She would have turned her back on Benvenuto Cellini if he was not 22 carats fine. She despised water-colour art; her conception of a picture was a vast domain of oily brown by an Old Master. The Babbages at the Hall had a display of gold plate swaggering in the corner of the dining-room; and the visitor (restrained by a plush rope from examining the workmanship) was told the value, and so passed on. I like my art unadorned: thought and skill, and the other strange quality that is added thereto, to make things beautiful—and nothing more. A farthing's worth of paint and paper, and, behold! a thing of beauty!—as they do in Japan. And if it should fall into the fire—well, it has gone like yesterday's sunset, and to-morrow there will be another.

These Japanese are indeed the apostles of cheapness. The Greeks lived to teach the world beauty, the Hebrews to teach it morality, and now the Japanese are hammering in the lesson that men may be honourable, daily life delightful, and a nation great without either freestone houses, marble mantelpieces, or mahogany sideboards. I have sometimes wished that my Aunt Charlotte could have travelled among the Japanese nation. She would, I know, have called it a "parcel of trash." Their use of paper—paper suits, paper pocket-handkerchiefs—would have made her rigid with contempt. I have tried, but I cannot imagine my Aunt Charlotte in paper underclothing. Her aversion to paper was extraordinary. Her Book of Beauty was printed on satin, and all her books were bound in leather, the boards regulated rather than decorated with a severe oblong. Her proper sphere was among the ancient Babylonians, among which massive populace even the newspapers were built of brick. She would have compared with the King's daughter whose raiment was of wrought gold. When I was a little boy I used to think she had a mahogany skeleton. However, she is gone, poor old lady, and at least she left me her furniture. Her ghost was torn in pieces after the sale—must have been. Even the old china went this way and that. I took what was perhaps a mean revenge of her for the innumerable black-holeings, bread-and-water dinners, summary chastisements, and impossible tasks she inflicted upon me for offences against her too solid possessions. You will see it at Woking. It is a light and graceful cross. It is a mere speck of white between the monstrous granite paperweights that oppress the dead on either side of her. Sometimes I am half sorry for that. When the end comes I shall not care to look her in the face—she will be so humiliated.

THE TROUBLE OF LIFE

I do not know whether this will awaken a sympathetic lassitude in, say, fifty per cent. of its readers, or whether my experience is unique and my testimony simply curious. At anyrate, it is as true as I can make it. Whether this is a mere mood, and a certain flagrant exhilaration my true attitude towards things, or this is my true attitude and the exuberant phase a lapse from it, I cannot say. Probably it does not matter. The thing is that I find life an extremely troublesome affair. I do not want to make any railing accusations against life; it is—to my taste—neither very sad nor very horrible. At times it is distinctly amusing. Indeed, I know nothing in the same line that can quite compare with it. But there is a difference between general appreciation and uncritical acceptance. At times I find life a Bother.

The kind of thing that I object to is, as a good example, all the troublesome things one has to do every morning in getting up. There is washing. This is an age of unsolicited personal confidences, and I will frankly confess that if it were not for Euphemia I do not think I should wash at all. There is a vast amount of humbug about washing. Vulgar people not only profess a passion for the practice, but a physical horror of being unwashed. It is a sort of cant. I can understand a sponge bath being a novelty the first time and exhilarating the second and third. But day after day, week after week, month after month, and nothing to show at the end of it all! Then there is shaving. I have to get shaved because Euphemia hates me with a blue jowl, and I will admit I hate myself. Yet, if I were left alone, I

H. G. Wells

do not think my personal taste would affect my decision; I will say that for myself. Either I hack about with a blunt razor—my razors are always blunt—until I am a kind of Whitechapel Horror, and with hair in tufts upon my chin like the top of a Bosjesman's head, or else I have to spend all the morning being dabbed about the face by a barber with damp hands. In either case it is a repulsive thing to have, eating into one's time when one might be living; and I have calculated that all the hair I have lost in this way, put end to end, would reach to Berlin. All that vital energy thrown away! However, "Thorns and bristles shall it bring forth to thee." I suppose it is part of the primal curse, and I try and stand it like a man. But the thing is a bother all the same.

Then after shaving comes the hunt for the collar-stud. Of all idiotic inventions the modern collar is the worst. A man who has to write things for such readers as mine cannot think over-night of where he puts his collar-stud; he has to keep his mind at an altogether higher level. Consequently he walks about the bedroom, thinking hard, and dropping things about: here a vest and there a collar, and sowing a bitter harvest against the morning. Or he sits on the edge of the bed jerking his garments this way and that. "I shot a slipper in the air," as the poet sings, and in the morning it turns up in the most impossible quarters, and where you least expect it. And, talking of going to bed, before Euphemia took the responsibility over, I was always forgetting to wind my watch. But now that is one of the things she neglects.

Then, after getting up, there is breakfast. Autolycus of the *Pall Mall Gazette* may find heaven there, but I am differently constituted. There is, to begin with the essence of the offence—the stuff that has to be eaten somehow. Then there is the paper. Unless it is the face of a fashionable beauty, I know of nothing more absolutely uninteresting than a morning paper. You always expect to find something in it, and never do. It wastes half my morning sometimes, going over and over the thing, and trying to find out why they publish it. If I edited a daily I think I should do like my father does when he writes to me. "Things much the same," he writes; "the usual fussing about the curate's red socks"—a long letter for him. The rest margin. And, by the bye, there are letters every morning at breakfast, too!

Now I do not grumble at letters. You can read them instead of getting on with your breakfast. They are entertaining in a way, and you can tear them up at the end, and in that respect at least they are better than people who come to see you. Usually, too, you need not make a reply. But sometimes Euphemia gets hold of some still untorn, and says in her dictatorial way that they *have* to be answered—insists—says I *must*. Yet she knows that nothing fills me with a livelier horror than having to answer letters. It paralyses me. I waste whole days sometimes mourning over the time that I shall have to throw away presently, answering some needless impertinence—requests for me to return books lent to me; reminders from the London Library that my subscription is overdue; proposals for me to renew my ticket at the stores—Euphemia's business really; invitations for me to go and be abashed before impertinent distinguished people: all kinds of bothering things.

And speaking of letters and invitations brings me round to friends. I dislike most people; in London they get in one's way in the street and fill up railway carriages, and in the country they stare at you—but I *hate* my friends. Yet Euphemia says I *must* "keep up" my friends. They would be all very well if they were really true friends and respected my feelings and left me alone, just to sit quiet. But they come wearing shiny clothes, and mop and mow at me and expect me to answer their gibberings. Polite conversation always appears to me to be a wicked perversion of the blessed gift of speech, which, I take it, was given us to season our lives rather than to make them insipid. New friends are the worst in this respect. With old friends one is more at home; you give them something to eat or drink, or look at, or something—whatever they seem to want—and just turn round and go on smoking quietly. But every now and then Euphemia or Destiny inflicts a new human being upon me. I do not mean a baby, though the

H. G. Wells

sentence has got that turn somehow, but an introduction; and the wretched thing, all angles and offence, keeps bobbing about me and discovering new ways of worrying me, trying, I believe, to find out what topics interest me, though the fact is no topics interest me. Once or twice, of course, I have met human beings I think I could have got on with very well, after a time; but in this mood, at least, I doubt if any human being is quite worth the bother of a new acquaintance.

These are just sample bothers—shaving, washing, answering letters, talking to people. I could specify hundreds more. Indeed, in my sadder moments, it seems to me life is all compact of bothers. There are the details of business— knowing the date approximately (an incessant anxiety) and the time of day. Then, having to buy things. Euphemia does most of this, it is true, but she draws the line at my boots and gloves and hosiery and tailoring. Then, doing up parcels and finding pieces of string or envelopes or stamps—which Euphemia might very well manage for me. Then, finding your way back after a quiet, thoughtful walk. Then, having to get matches for your pipe. I sometimes dream of a better world, where pipe, pouch, and matches all keep together instead of being mutually negatory. But Euphemia is always putting everything into some hiding-hole or other, which she calls its "place." Trivial things in their way, you may say, yet each levying so much toll on my brain and nervous system, and demanding incessant vigilance and activity. I calculated once that I wasted a masterpiece upon these mountainous little things about every three months of my life. Can I help thinking of them, then, and asking why I suffer thus? And can I avoid seeing at last how it is they hang together?

For there is still one other bother, a kind of *bother botherum*, to tell of, though I hesitate at the telling. It brings this rabble herd of worries into line and makes them formidable; it is, so to speak, the Bother Commander-in-Chief. Well! Euphemia. I simply worship the ground she treads upon, mind, but at the same time the truth is the truth. Euphemia is a bother. She is a brave little woman, and helps me in every conceivable way.

But I wish she would not. It is so obviously all her doing. She makes me get up of a morning—I would not stand as much from anybody else—and keeps a sharp eye on my chin and collar. If it were not for her I could sit about always with no collar or tie on in that old jacket she gave to the tramp, and just smoke and grow a beard and let all the bothers slide. I would never wash, never shave, never answer any letters, never go to see any friends, never do any work—except, perhaps, an insulting postcard to a publisher now and again. I would just sit about.

Sometimes I think this may be peculiar in me. At other times I fancy I am giving voice to the secret feeling of every member of my sex. I suspect, then, that we would all do as the noble savage does, take our things off and lie about comfortable, if only someone had the courage to begin. It is these women—all love and reverence to Euphemia notwithstanding—who make us work and bother us with Things. They keep us decent, and remind us we have a position to support. And really, after all, this is not my original discovery! There is the third chapter of Genesis, for instance. And then who has not read Carlyle's gloating over a certain historical suit of leather? It gives me a queer thrill of envy, that Quaker Fox and his suit of leather. Conceive it, if you can! One would never have to quail under the scrutiny of a tailor any more. Thoreau, too, come to think of it, was, by way of being a prophet, a pioneer in this Emancipation of Man from Bothery.

Then the silent gentry who brew our Chartreuse; what are they in retirement for? Looking back into history, with the glow of discovery in my eyes, I find records of wise men—everyone acknowledged they were wise men—who lived apart. In every age the same associate of solitude, silence, and wisdom. The holy hermits!... I grant it, they professed to flee wickedness and seek after righteousness, but now my impression is that they fled bothers. We all know they had an intense aversion to any savour of domesticity, and they never shaved, washed, dined, visited, had new clothes. Holiness, indeed! They were *viveurs*.... We have witnessed Religion without Theology, and why not an Unsectarian Thebaid? I sometimes fancy it needs only one brave man to begin.... If it were not for the fuss Euphemia would make I certainly should. But I know she would come and worry me worse than St. Anthony was worried until I put them all on again, and that keeps me from the attempt.

I am curious whether mine is the common experience. I fancy, after all, I am only seeing in a clearer way, putting into modern phrase, so to speak, an observation old as the Pentateuch. And looking up I read upon a little almanac with which Euphemia has cheered my desk:—

"The world was sad" (sweet sadness!)
"The garden was a wild" (a picturesque wild)
"And man the hermit" (he made no complaint)
"Till the woman smiled."—CAMPBELL.

[And very shortly after he had, as you know, all that bother about the millinery.]

ON THE CHOICE OF A WIFE

Wife-choosing is an unending business. This sounds immoral, but what I mean will be clearer in the context. People have lived—innumerable people—exhausted experience, and yet other people keep on coming to hand, none the wiser, none the better. It is like a waterfall more than anything else in the world. Every year one has to turn to and warn another batch about these stale old things. Yet it is one's duty—the last thing that remains to a man. And as a piece of worldly wisdom, that has nothing to do with wives, always leave a few duties neglected for the comfort of your age. There are such a lot of other things one can do when one is young.

Now, the kind of wife a young fellow of eight- or nine-and-twenty insists on selecting is something of one-and-twenty or less, inexperienced, extremely pretty, graceful, and well dressed, not too clever, accomplished; but I need not go on, for the youthful reader can fill in the picture himself from his own ideal. Every young man has his own ideal, as a matter of course, and they are all exactly alike. Now, I do not intend to repeat all the stale old saws of out-of-date wiseacres. Most of them are even more foolish than the follies they reprove. Take, for instance, the statement that "beauty fades." Absurd; everyone knows perfectly well that, as the years creep on, beauty simply gets more highly coloured. And then, "beauty is only skin-deep." Fantastically wrong! Some of it is not that; and, for the rest, is a woman like a toy balloon?—just a surface? To hear that proverb from a man is to know him at once for a phonographic kind of fool. The fundamental and

H. G. Wells

enduring grace of womanhood goes down to the skeleton; you cannot have a pretty face without a pretty skull, just as you cannot have one without a good temper.

Yet all the same there is an excellent reason why one should shun beauty in a prospective wife, at anyrate obvious beauty—the kind of beauty people talk about, and which gets into the photographers' windows. The common beautiful woman has a style of her own, a favourite aspect. After all, she cannot be perfect. She comes upon you, dazzles you, marries you; there is a time of ecstasy. People envy you, continue to envy you. After a time you envy yourself—yourself of the day before yesterday. For the imperfection, the inevitable imperfection—in one case I remember it was a smile—becomes visible to you, becomes your especial privilege. That is the real reason. No beauty is a beauty to her husband. But with the plain woman—the thoroughly plain woman—it is different. At first—I will not mince matters—her ugliness is an impenetrable repulse. Face it. After a time little things begin to appear through the violent discords: little scraps of melody—a shy tenderness in her smile that peeps out at you and vanishes, a something that is winning, looking out of her eyes. You find a waviness of her hair that you never saw at the beginning, a certain surprising, pleasing, enduring want of clumsiness in part of her ear. And it is yours. You can see she strikes the beholder with something of a shock; and while the beauty of the beauty is common for all the world to rejoice in, you will find in your dear, plain wife beauty enough and to spare; exquisite—for it is all your own, your treasure-trove, your safely-hidden treasure....

Then, in the matter of age; though young fellows do not imagine it, it is very easy to marry a wife too young. Marriage has been defined as a foolish bargain in which one man provides for another man's daughter, but there is no reason why this should go so far as completing her education. If your conception of happiness is having something pretty and innocent and troublesome about you, something that you can cherish and make happy, a pet rabbit is in every way preferable. At the worst that will nibble your boots. I have known several cases of the girl-wife, and it always began like an idyll, charmingly; the tenderest care on one hand, winsome worship on the other—until some little thing, a cut chin or a missing paper, startled the pure and natural man out of his veneer, dancing and blaspheming, with the most amazing consequences. Only a proven saint should marry a girl-wife, and his motives might be misunderstood. The idyllic wife is a beautiful thing to read about, but in practice idylls should be kept episodes; in practice the idyllic life is a little too like a dinner that is all dessert. A common man, after a time, tires of winsome worship; he craves after companionship, and a sympathy based on experience. The ordinary young man, with the still younger wife, I have noticed, continues to love her with all his heart—and spends his leisure telling somebody else's wife all about it. If in these days of blatant youth an experienced man's counsel is worth anything, it would be to marry a woman considerably older than oneself, if one must marry at all. And while upon this topic—and I have lived long —the ideal wife, I am persuaded, from the close observation of many years, is invariably, by some mishap, a widow....

Avoid social charm. It was the capacity for entertaining visitors that ruined Paradise. It grows upon a woman. An indiscriminating personal magnetism is perhaps the most dreadful vice a wife can have. You think you have married the one woman in the world, and you find you have married a host—that is to say, a hostess. Instead of making a home for you she makes you something between an ethnographical museum and a casual ward. You find your rooms littered with people and teacups and things, strange creatures that no one could possibly care for, that seem scarcely to care for themselves. You go about the house treading upon chance geniuses, and get tipped by inexperienced guests. And even when she does not entertain, she is continually going out. I do not deny that charming people are charming, that their company should be sought, but seeking it in marriage is an altogether different matter.

Then, I really must insist that young men do not understand the real truth about accomplishments. There comes a day when the most variegated wife comes to the end of her tunes, and another when she ends them for the second time; *Vita longa, ars brevis*—at least, as regards the art of the schoolgirl. It is only like marrying a slightly more complicated barrel-organ. And, for another point, watch the young person you would honour with your hand for the slightest inkling of economy or tidiness. Young men are so full of poetry and emotion that it does not occur to them how widely the sordid vices are distributed in the other sex. If you are a hotel proprietor, or a school proprietor, or a day labourer, such weaknesses become a strength, of course, but not otherwise. For a literary person—if perchance you are a literary person—it is altogether too dreadful. You are always getting swept and garnished, straightened up and sent out to be shaved. And home—even your study—becomes a glittering, spick-and-span mechanism. But you know the parable of the seven devils?

To conclude, a summary. The woman you choose should be plain, as plain as you can find, as old or older than yourself, devoid of social gifts or accomplishments, poor—for your self-respect—and with a certain amiable untidiness. Of course no young man will heed this, but at least I have given my counsel, and very excellent reasons for that counsel. And possibly I shall be able to remind him that I told him as much, in the course of a few years' time. And, by the bye, I had almost forgotten! Never by any chance marry a girl whose dresses do up at the back, unless you can afford her a maid or so of her own.

THE HOUSE OF DI SORNO

A MANUSCRIPT FOUND IN A BOX

And the box, Euphemia's. Brutally raided it was by an insensate husband, eager for a tie and too unreasonably impatient to wait an hour or so until she could get home and find it for him. There was, of course, no tie at all in that box, for all his stirring—as anyone might have known; but, if there was no tie, there were certain papers that at least suggested a possibility of whiling away the time until the Chooser and Distributer of Ties should return. And, after all, there is no reading like your accidental reading come upon unawares.

It was a discovery, indeed, that Euphemia *had* papers. At the first glance these close-written sheets suggested a treasonable Keynote, and the husband gripped it with a certain apprehension mingling with his relief at the opiate of reading. It was, so to speak, the privilege of police he exercised, so he justified himself. He began to read. But what is this? "She stood on the balcony outside the window, while the noblest-born in the palace waited on her every capricious glance, and watched for an unbending look to relieve her hauteur, but in vain." None of your snippy-snappy Keynote there!

Then he turned over a page or so of the copy, doubting if the privilege of police still held good. Standing out by virtue of a different ink, and coming immediately after "bear her to her proud father," were the words, "How many yards of carpet 3/4 yds. wide will cover room, width 16 ft., length 27-1/2 ft.?"

H. G. Wells

Then he knew he was in the presence of the great romance that Euphemia wrote when she was sixteen. He had heard something of it before. He held it doubtfully in his hands, for the question of conscience still troubled him. "Bah!" he said abruptly, "not to find it irresistible was to slight the authoress and her skill." And with that he sat plump down among the things in the box very comfortably and began reading, and, indeed, read until Euphemia arrived. But she, at the sight of his head and legs, made several fragmentary and presumably offensive remarks about crushing some hat or other, and proceeded with needless violence to get him out of the box again. However, that is my own private trouble. We are concerned now with the merits of Euphemia's romance.

The hero of the story is a Venetian, named (for some unknown reason) Ivan di Sorno. So far as I ascertained, he is the entire house of Di Sorno referred to in the title. No other Di Sornos transpired. Like others in the story, he is possessed of untold wealth, tempered by a profound sorrow, for some cause which remains unmentioned, but which is possibly internal. He is first displayed "pacing a sombre avenue of ilex and arbutus that reflected with singular truth the gloom of his countenance," and "toying sadly with the jewelled hilt of his dagger." He meditates upon his loveless life and the burthen of riches. Presently he "paces the long and magnificent gallery," where a "hundred generations of Di Sornos, each with the same flashing eye and the same marble brow, look down with the same sad melancholy upon the beholder"—a truly monotonous exhibition. It would be too much for anyone, day after day. He decides that he will travel. Incognito.

The next chapter is headed "In Old Madrid," and Di Sorno, cloaked to conceal his grandeur, "moves sad and observant among the giddy throng." But "Gwendolen"—the majestic Gwendolen of the balcony—"marked his pallid yet beautiful countenance." And the next day at the bull-fight she "flung her bouquet into the arena, and turning to Di Sorno"—a perfect stranger, mind you—"smiled commandingly." "In a moment he had flung himself headlong down among the flashing blades of the toreadors and the trampling confusion of bulls, and in another he stood before her, bowing low with the recovered flowers in his hand. 'Fair sir,' she said, 'methinks my poor flowers were scarce worth your trouble.'" A very proper remark. And then suddenly I put the manuscript down.

My heart was full of pity for Euphemia. Thus had she gone a-dreaming. A man of imposing physique and flashing eye, who would fling you oxen here and there, and vault in and out of an arena without catching a breath, for his lady's sake—and here I sat, the sad reality, a lean and slippered literary pretender, and constitutionally afraid of cattle.

Poor little Euphemia! For after all is said and done, and the New Woman gibed out of existence, I am afraid we do undeceive these poor wives of ours a little after the marrying is over. It may be they have deceived themselves, in the first place, but that scarcely affects their disappointment. These dream-lovers of theirs, these monsters of unselfishness and devotion, these tall fair Donovans and dark worshipping Wanderers! And then comes the rabble rout of us poor human men, damning at our breakfasts, wiping pens upon our coat sleeves, smelling of pipes, fearing our editors, and turning Euphemia's private boxes into public copy. And they take it so steadfastly—most of them. They never let us see the romance we have robbed them of, but turn to and make the best of it—and us—with such sweet grace. Only now and then—as in the instance of a flattened hat—may a cry escape them. And even then—

But a truce to reality! Let us return to Di Sorno.

This individual does not become enamoured of Gwendolen, as the crude novel reader might anticipate. He answers her "coldly," and his eye rests the while on her "tirewoman, the sweet Margot." Then come scenes of jealousy and love, outside a castle with heavily mullioned windows. The sweet Margot, though she turns out to be the daughter of a bankrupt prince, has one characteristic of your servant all the world over—she spends all her time looking out of the window. Di Sorno tells her of his love on the evening of the bull-fight, and she cheerfully promises to "learn to love him," and therafter he spends all his days and nights "spurring his fiery steed down the road" that leads by the castle containing the young scholar. It becomes a habit with him—in all, he does it seventeen times in three chapters. Then, "ere it is too late," he implores Margot to fly.

Gwendolen, after a fiery scene with Margot, in which she calls her a "petty minion,"—pretty language for a young gentle-woman,—"sweeps with unutterable scorn from the room," never, to the reader's huge astonishment, to appear in the story again, and Margot flies with Di Sorno to Grenada, where the Inquisition, consisting apparently of a single monk with a "blazing eye," becomes extremely machinatory. A certain Countess di Morno, who intends to marry Di Sorno, and who has been calling into the story in a casual kind of way since the romance began, now comes prominently forward. She has denounced Margot for heresy, and at a masked ball the Inquisition, disguised in a yellow domino, succeeds in separating the young couple, and in carrying off "the sweet Margot" to a convent.

"Di Sorno, half distraught, flung himself into a cab and drove to all the hotels in Grenada" (he overlooked the police station), and, failing to find Margot, becomes mad. He goes about ejaculating "Mad, mad!" than which nothing could be more eloquent of his complete mental inversion. In his paroxysms the Countess di Morno persuades him to "lead her to the altar," but on the way (with a certain indelicacy they go to church in the same conveyance) she lets slip a little secret. So Di Sorno jumps out of the carriage, "hurling the crowd apart," and, "flourishing his drawn sword," "clamoured at the gate of the Inquisition" for Margot. The Inquisition, represented by the fiery-eyed monk, "looked over the gate at him." No doubt it felt extremely uncomfortable.

Now it was just at this thrilling part that Euphemia came

home, and the trouble about the flattened hat began. I never flattened her hat. It was in the box, and so was I; but as for deliberate flattening—It was just a thing that happened. She should not write such interesting stories if she expects me to go on tiptoe through the world looking about for her hats. To have that story taken away just at that particular moment was horrible. There was fully as much as I had read still to come, so that a lot happened after this duel of Sword *v.* Fiery Eye. I know from a sheet that came out of place that Margot stabbed herself with a dagger ("richly jewelled"), but of all that came between I have not the faintest suspicion. That is the peculiar interest of it. At this particular moment the one book I want to read in all the world is the rest of this novel of Euphemia's. And simply, on the score of a new hat needed, she keeps it back and haggles!

OF CONVERSATION

AN APOLOGY

I must admit that in conversation I am not a brilliant success. Partly, indeed, that may be owing to the assiduity with which my aunt suppressed my early essays in the art: "Children," she said, "should be seen but not heard," and incontinently rapped my knuckles. To a larger degree, however, I regard it as intrinsic. This tendency to silence, to go out of the rattle and dazzle of the conversation into a quiet apart, is largely, I hold, the consequence of a certain elevation and breadth and tenderness of mind; I am no blowfly to buzz my way through the universe, no rattle that I should be expected to delight my fellow-creatures by the noises I produce. I go about to this social function and that, deporting myself gravely and decently in silence, taking, if possible, a back seat; and, in consequence of that, people who do not understand me have been heard to describe me as a "stick," as "shy," and by an abundance of the like unflattering terms. So that I am bound almost in self-justification to set down my reasons for this temperance of mine in conversation.

Speech, no doubt, is a valuable gift, but at the same time it is a gift that may be abused. What is regarded as polite conversation is, I hold, such an abuse. Alcohol, opium, tea, are all very excellent things in their way; but imagine continuous alcohol, an incessant opium, or to receive, ocean-like, a perennially flowing river of tea! That is my objection to this conversation: its continuousness. You have to keep on. You find three or four people gathered together, and instead of being restful and recreative, sitting in comfortable attitudes and at peace with themselves and each other, and now and again, perhaps three or four times in an hour, making a worthy and memorable remark, they are all haggard and intent upon keeping this fetish flow agoing. A fortuitous score of cows in a field are a thousand times happier than a score of people deliberately assembled for the purposes of happiness. These conversationalists say the most shallow and needless of things, impart aimless information, simulate interest they do not feel, and generally impugn their claim to be considered reasonable creatures. Why, when people assemble without hostile intentions, it should be so imperative to keep the trickling rill of talk running, I find it impossible to imagine. It is a vestige of the old barbaric times, when men murdered at sight for a mere whim; when it was good form to take off your sword in the antechamber, and give your friend your dagger-hand, to show him it was no business visit. Similarly, you keep up this babblement to show your mind has no sinister concentration, not necessarily because you have anything to say, but as a guarantee of good faith. You have to make a noise all the time, like the little boy who was left in the room with the plums. It is the only possible explanation.

To a logical mind there is something very distressing in this social law of gabble. Out of regard for Mrs. A, let us say, I attend some festival she has inaugurated. There I meet for the first time a young person of pleasant exterior, and I am placed in her company to deliver her at a dinner-table, or dance her about, or keep her out of harm's way, in a cosy nook. She has also never seen me before, and probably does not want particularly to see me now. However, I find her nice to look at, and she has taken great pains to make herself nice to look at, and why we cannot pass the evening, I looking at her and she being looked at, I cannot imagine. But no; we must talk. Now, possibly there are topics she knows about and I do not—it is unlikely, but suppose so; on these topics she requires no information. Again, I know about other topics things unknown to her, and it seems a mean and priggish thing to broach these,

H. G. Wells

since they put her at a disadvantage. Thirdly, comes a last group of subjects upon which we are equally informed, and upon which, therefore, neither of us is justified in telling things to the other. This classification of topics seems to me exhaustive.

These considerations, I think, apply to all conversations. In every conversation, every departure must either be a presumption when you talk into your antagonist's special things, a pedantry when you fall back upon your own, or a platitude when you tell each other things you both know. I don't see any other line a conversation can take. The reason why one has to keep up the stream of talk is possibly, as I have already suggested, to manifest goodwill. And in so many cases this could be expressed so much better by a glance, a deferential carriage, possibly in some cases a gentle pressure of the hand, or a quiet persistent smile. And suppose there is some loophole in my reasoning—though I cannot see it—and that possible topics exist, how superficial and unexact is the best conversation to a second-rate book!

Even with two people you see the objection, but when three or four are gathered together the case is infinitely worse to a man of delicate perceptions. Let us suppose—I do not grant it—that there is a possible sequence of things to say to the person A that really harmonise with A and yourself. Grant also that there is a similar sequence between yourself and B. Now, imagine yourself and A and B at the corners of an equilateral triangle set down to talk to each other. The kind of talk that A appreciates is a discord with B, and similarly B's sequence is impossible in the hearing of A. As a matter of fact, a real conversation of three people is the most impossible thing in the world. In real life one of the three always drops out and becomes a mere audience, or a mere partisan. In real life you and A talk, and B pretends to be taking a share by interjecting interruptions, or one of the three talks a monologue. And the more subtle your sympathy and the greater your restraint from self-assertion, the more incredible triple and quadruple conversation becomes.

I have observed that there is even nowadays a certain advance towards my views in this matter. Men may not pick out antagonists, and argue to the general audience as once they did: there is a tacit taboo of controversy, neither may you talk your "shop," nor invite your antagonist to talk his. There is also a growing feeling against extensive quotations or paraphrases from the newspapers. Again, personalities, scandal, are, at least in theory, excluded. This narrows the scope down to the "last new book," "the last new play," "impressions de voyage," and even here it is felt that any very ironical or satirical remarks, anything unusual, in fact, may disconcert your adversary. You ask: Have you read the *Wheels of Chance*? The answer is "Yes." "Do you like it?" "A little vulgar, I thought." And so forth. Most of this is stereo. It is akin to responses in church, a prescription, a formula. And, following out this line of thought, I have had a vision of the twentieth century dinner. At a distance it is very like the nineteenth century type; the same bright light, the same pleasant deglutition, the same hum of conversation; but, approaching, you discover each diner has a little drum-shaped body under his chin—his phonograph. So he dines and babbles at his ease. In the smoking-room he substitutes his anecdote record. I imagine, too, the suburban hostess meeting the new maiden: "I hope, dear, you have brought a lot of conversation," just as now she asks for the music. For my own part, I must confess I find this dinner conversation particularly a bother. If I could eat with my eye it would be different.

I lose a lot of friends through this conversational difficulty. They think it is my dulness or my temper, when really it is only my refined mind, my subtlety of consideration. It seems to me that when I go to see a man, I go to see him—to enjoy his presence. If he is my friend, the sight of him healthy and happy is enough for me. I don't want him to keep his vocal cords, and I don't want to keep my own vocal cords, in incessant vibration all the time I am in his company. If I go to see a man, it distracts me to have to talk and it distracts me to hear him talking. I can't imagine why one should not go and sit about in people's rooms, without bothering them and without their bothering you to say all these stereotyped things. Quietly go in, sit down, look at your man until you have seen him enough, and then go. Why not?

Let me once more insist that this keeping up a conversation is a sign of insecurity, of want of confidence. All those who have had real friends know that when the friendship is assured the gabble ceases. You are not at the heart of your friend, if either of you cannot go off comfortably to sleep in the other's presence. Speech was given us to make known our needs, and for imprecation, expostulation, and entreaty. This pitiful necessity we are under, upon social occasions, to say something—however inconsequent—is, I am assured, the very degradation of speech.

IN A LITERARY HOUSEHOLD

In the literary household of fiction and the drama, things are usually in a distressing enough condition. The husband, as you know, has a hacking cough, and the wife a dying baby, and they write in the intervals of these cares among the litter of the breakfast things. Occasionally a comic, but sympathetic, servant brings in an armful—"heaped up and brimming over"—of rejected MSS., for, in the dramatic life, it never rains but it pours. Instead of talking about editors in a bright and vigorous fashion, as the recipients of rejections are wont, the husband groans and covers his face with his hands, and the wife, leaving the touching little story she is writing—she posts this about 9 p.m., and it brings in a publisher and L100 or so before 10.30—comforts him by flopping suddenly over his shoulder. "Courage," she says, stroking his hyacinthine locks (whereas all real literary men are more or less grey or bald). Sometimes, as in *Our Flat*, comic tradesmen interrupt the course of true literature with their ignoble desire for cash payment, and sometimes, as in *Our Boys*, uncles come and weep at the infinite pathos of a bad breakfast egg. But it's always a very sordid, dusty, lump-in-your-throaty affair, and no doubt it conduces to mortality by deterring the young and impressionable from literary vices. As for its truth, that is another matter altogether.

Yet it must not be really imagined that a literary household is just like any other. There is the brass paper-fastener, for instance. I have sometimes thought that Euphemia married me with an eye to these conveniences. She has two in her grey

H. G. Wells

gloves, and one (with the head inked) in her boot in the place of a button. Others I suspect her of. Then she fastened the lamp shade together with them, and tried one day to introduce them instead of pearl buttons as efficient anchorage for cuffs and collars. And she made a new handle for the little drawer under the inkstand with one. Indeed, the literary household is held together, so to speak, by paper-fasteners, and how other people get along without them we are at a loss to imagine.

And another point, almost equally important, is that the husband is generally messing about at home. That is, indeed, to a superficial observer, one of the most remarkable characteristics of the literary household. Other husbands are cast out in the morning to raven for income and return to a home that is swept and garnished towards the end of the day; but the literary husband is ever in possession. His work must not be disturbed even when he is merely thinking. The study is consequently a kind of domestic cordite factory, and you are never certain when it may explode. The concussion of a dustpan and brush may set it going, the sweeping of a carpet in the room upstairs. Then behold a haggard, brain-weary man, fierce and dishevelled, and full of shattered masterpiece—expostulating. Other houses have their day of cleaning out this room, and their day for cleaning out that; but in the literary household there is one uniform date for all such functions, and that is "to-morrow." So that Mrs. Mergles makes her purifying raids with her heart in her mouth, and has acquired a way of leaving the pail and brush, or whatever artillery she has with her, in a manner that unavoidably engages the infuriated brute's attention and so covers her retreat.

It is a problem that has never been probably solved, this discord of order and orderly literary work. Possibly it might be done by making the literary person live elsewhere or preventing literary persons from having households. However it might be done, it is not done. This is a thing innocent girls exposed to the surreptitious proposals of literary men do not understand. They think it will be very fine to have photographs of themselves and their "cosy nooks" published in magazines, to illustrate the man's interviews, and the full horror of having this feral creature always about the house, and scarcely ever being able to do any little thing without his knowing it, is not brought properly home to them until escape is impossible.

And then there is the taint of "copy" everywhere. That is really the fundamental distinction. It is the misfortune of literary people, that they have to write about something. There is no reason, of course, why they should, but the thing is so. Consequently, they are always looking about them for something to write about. They cannot take a pure-minded interest in anything in earth or heaven. Their servant is no servant, but a character; their cat is a possible reservoir of humorous observation; they look out of window and see men as columns walking. Even the sanctity of their own hearts, their self-respect, their most private emotions are disregarded. The wife is infected with the taint. Her private opinion of her husband she makes into a short story—forgets its origin and shows it him with pride—while the husband decants his heart-beats into occasional verse and minor poetry. It is amazing what a lot of latter-day literature consists of such breaches of confidence. And not simply latter-day literature.

The visitor is fortunate who leaves no marketable impression behind. The literary entertainers eye you over, as if they were dealers in a slave mart, and speculate on your uses. They try to think how you would do as a scoundrel, and mark your little turns of phrase and kinks of thought to that end. The innocent visitor bites his cake and talks about theatres, while the meditative person in the arm-chair may be in imagination stabbing him, or starving him on a desert island, or even—horrible to tell!—flinging him headlong into the arms of the young lady to the right and "covering her face with a thousand passionate kisses." A manuscript in the rough of Euphemia's, that I recently suppressed, was an absolutely scandalous example of this method of utilising one's acquaintances. Mrs. Harborough, who was indeed Euphemia's most confidential friend for six weeks and more, she had made to elope with

Scrimgeour—as steady and honourable a man as we know, though unpleasant to Euphemia on account of his manner of holding his teacup. I believe there really was something—quite harmless, of course—between Mrs. Harborough and Scrimgeour, and that, imparted in confidence, had been touched up with vivid colour here and there and utilised freely. Scrimgeour is represented as always holding teacups in his peculiar way, so that anyone would recognise him at once. Euphemia calls that character. Then Harborough, who is really on excellent terms with his wife, and, in spite of his quiet manner, a very generous and courageous fellow, is turned aside from his headlong pursuit of the fugitives across Wimbledon Common— they elope, by the bye, on Scrimgeour's tandem bicycle—by the fear of being hit by a golf ball. I pointed out to Euphemia that these things were calculated to lose us friends, and she promises to destroy the likeness; but I have no confidence in her promise. She will probably clap a violent auburn wig on Mrs. Harborough and make Scrimgeour squint and give Harborough a big beard. The point that she won't grasp is, that with that fatal facility for detail, which is one of the most indisputable proofs of woman's intellectual inferiority, she has reproduced endless remarks and mannerisms of these excellent people with more than photographic fidelity. But this is really a private trouble, though it illustrates very well the shameless way in which those who have the literary taint will bring to market their most intimate affairs.

ON SCHOOLING AND THE PHASES OF
MR. SANDSOME

I do not know if you remember your "dates." Indeed, I do not know if anyone does. My own memory is of a bridge; like that bridge of Goldsmith's, standing firm and clear on its hither piers and then passing into a cloud. In the beginning of days was "William the Conqueror, 1066," and the path lay safe and open to Henry the Second; then came Titanic forms of kings, advancing and receding, elongating and dwindling, exchanging dates, losing dates, stealing dates from battles and murders and great enactments—even inventing dates, vacant years that were really no dates at all. The things I have suffered—prisons, scourgings, beating with rods, wild masters, in bounds often, a hundred lines often, standing on forms and holding out books often—on account of these dates! I knew, and knew well before I was fifteen, what these "heredity" babblers are only beginning to discover—that the past is the curse of the present. But I never knew my dates—never. And I marvel now that all little boys do not grow up to be Republicans, seeing how much they suffer for the mere memory of Kings.

Then there were pedigrees, and principal parts and conjugations, and county towns. Every county had a county town, and it was always on a river. Mr. Sandsome never allowed us a town without that colophon. I remember in my early manhood going to Guildford on the Wey, and trying to find that unobtrusive rivulet. I went over the downs for miles. It is not only the Wey I have had a difficulty in finding. There are certain verses—Heaven help me, but I have forgotten

H. G. Wells

them!—about "*i* vel *e* dat" (*was* it dat?) "utrum malis"—if I remember rightly—and all that about *amo, amas, amat*. There was a multitude of such things I acquired, and they lie now, in the remote box-rooms and lumber recesses of my mind, a rusting armoury far gone in decay. I have never been able to find a use for them. I wonder even now why Mr. Sandsome equipped me with them. Yet he seemed to be in deadly earnest about this learning, and I still go in doubt. In those early days he impressed me, chiefly in horizontal strips, with the profoundest respect for his mental and physical superiority. I credited him then, and still incline to believe he deserved to be credited, with a sincere persuasion that unless I learnt these things I should assuredly go—if I may be frank—to the devil. It may be so. I may be living in a fool's paradise, prospering—like that wicked man the Psalmist disliked. Some unsuspected gulf may open, some undreamt-of danger thrust itself through the phantasmagoria of the universe, and I may learn too late the folly of forgetting my declensions.

I remember Mr. Sandsome chiefly as sitting at his desk, in a little room full of boys, a humming hive whose air was thick with dust, as the slanting sunbeams showed. When we were not doing sums or writing copies, we were always learning or saying lessons. In the early morning Mr. Sandsome sat erect and bright, his face animated, his ruddy eyes keen and observant, the cane hanging but uncertainly upon its hook. There was a standing up of classes, a babble of repetition, now and then a crisis. How long the days were then! I have heard that scientific people—Professor C. Darwin is their leader, unless I err—which probably I do, for names and dates I have hated from my youth up—say the days grow longer. Anyhow, whoever says it, it is quite wrong. But as the lank hours of that vast schooltime drawled on, Mr. Sandsome lost energy, drooped like a flower,—especially if the day was at all hot,—his sandy hair became dishevelled, justice became nerveless, hectic, and hasty. Finally came copybooks; and yawns and weird rumblings from Mr. Sandsome. And so the world aged to the dinner-hour.

When I had been home—it was a day school, for my aunt, who had an appetite for such things, knew that boarding-schools were sinks of iniquity—and returned, I had Mr. Sandsome at another phase. He had dined—for we were simple country folk. The figurative suggestions of that "phase" are irresistible—the lunar quality. May I say that Mr. Sandsome was at his full? We now stood up, thirty odd of us altogether, to read, reading out of books in a soothing monotone, and he sat with his reading-book before him, ruddy as the setting sun, and slowly, slowly settling down. But now and then he would jerk back suddenly into staring wakefulness as though he were fishing—with himself as bait—for school-boy crimes in the waters of oblivion—and fancied a nibble. That was a dangerous time, full of anxiety. At last he went right under and slept, and the reading grew cheerful, full of quaint glosses and unexpected gaps, leaping playfully from boy to boy, instead of travelling round with a proper decorum. But it never ceased, and little Hurkley's silly little squeak of a voice never broke in upon its mellow flow. (It took a year for Hurkley's voice to break.) Any such interruption and Mr. Sandsome woke up and into his next phase forthwith—a disagreeable phase always, and one we made it our business to postpone as long as possible.

During that final period, the last quarter, Mr. Sandsome was distinctly malignant. It was hard to do right; harder still to do wrong. A feverish energy usually inspired our government. "Let us try to get some work done," Mr. Sandsome would say—and I have even known him teach things then. More frequently, with a needless bitterness, he set us upon impossible tasks, demanding a colossal tale of sums perhaps, scattering pens and paper and sowing the horrors of bookkeeping, or chastising us with the scorpions of parsing and translation. And even in wintry weather the little room grew hot and stuffy, and we terminated our schoolday, much exhausted, with minds lax, lounging attitudes, and red ears. What became of Mr. Sandsome after the giving-out of home-work, the concluding prayer, and the aftermath of impositions, I do not know. I stuffed my books, such as came to hand—very dirty they were inside, and very neat out with my Aunt Charlotte's chintz covers—into my green baize bag, and went forth from the mysteries of schooling into the great world, up the broad white road that went slanting over the Down.

I say "the mysteries of schooling" deliberately. I wondered then, I wonder still, what it was all for. Reading, almost my only art, I learnt from Aunt Charlotte; a certain facility in drawing I acquired at home and took to school, to my own undoing. "Undoing," again, is deliberate—it was no mere swish on the hand, gentle reader. But the things I learnt, more or less partially, at school, lie in my mind, like the "Sarsen" stones of Wiltshire—great, disconnected, time-worn chunks amidst the natural herbage of it. "The Rivers of the East Coast; the Tweed, the Tyne, the Wear, the Tees, the Humber"—why is that, for instance, sticking up among my ferns and wild flowers? It is not only useless but misleading, for the Humber is not another Tweed. I sometimes fancy the world may be mad—yet that seems egotistical. The fact remains that for the greater part of my young life Mr. Sandsome got an appetite upon us from nine till twelve, and digested his dinner, at first placidly and then with petulance, from two until five—and we thirty odd boys were sent by our twenty odd parents to act as a sort of chorus to his physiology. And he was fed (as I judge) more than sufficiently, clothed, sheltered, and esteemed on account of this relation. I think, after all, there must have been something in that schooling. I can't believe the world mad. And I have forgotten it—or as good as forgotten it—all! At times I feel a wild impulse to hunt up all those chintz-covered books, and brush up my dates and paradigms, before it is too late.

THE POET AND THE EMPORIUM

"I am beginning life," he said, with a sigh. "Great Heavens! I have spent a day—*a day!*—in a shop. Three bedroom suites and a sideboard are among the unanticipated pledges of our affection. Have you lithia? For a man of twelve limited editions this has been a terrible day."

I saw to his creature comforts. His tie was hanging outside his waistcoat, and his complexion was like white pasteboard that has got wet. "Courage," said I. "It will not occur again—"

"It will," said he. "We have to get there again tomorrow. We have—what is it?—carpets, curtains—"

He produced his tablets. I was amazed. Those receptacles of choice thoughts!

"The amber sunlight splashing through the leaky—leafy interlacing green," he read. "No!—that's not it. Ah, here! Curtains! Drawing-room—not to cost more than thirty shillings! And there's all the Kitchen Hardware! (Thanks.) Dining-room chairs—query—rush bottoms? What's this? G.L.I.S.—ah! "Glistering thro' deeps of glaucophane"—that's nothing. Mem. to see can we afford Indian needlework chairs—57s. 6d.? It's dreadful, Bellows!"

He helped himself to a cigarette.

"Find the salesman pleasant?" said I.

H. G. Wells

"Delightful. Assumed I was a spendthrift millionaire at first. Produced in an off-hand way an eighty-guinea bedroom suite—we're trying to do the entire business, you know, on about two hundred pounds. Well—that's ten editions, you know. Came down, with evidently dwindling respect, to things that were still ruinously expensive. I told him we wanted an idyll—love in a cottage, and all that kind of thing. He brushed that on one side, said idols were upstairs in the Japanese Department, and that perhaps we might *do* with a servant's set of bedroom furniture. Do with a set! He was a gloomy man with (I should judge) some internal pain. I tried to tell him that there was quite a lot of middle-class people like myself in the country, people of limited or precarious means, whose existence he seemed to ignore; assured him some of them led quite beautiful lives. But he had no ideas beyond wardrobes. I quite forgot the business of shopping in an attempt to kindle a little human enthusiasm in his heart. We were in a great vast place full of wardrobes, with a remote glittering vista of brass bedsteads—skeleton beds, you know—and I tried to inspire him with some of the poetry of his emporium; tried to make him imagine these beds and things going east and west, north and south, to take sorrow, servitude, joy, worry, failing strength, restless ambition in their impartial embraces. He only turned round to Annie, and asked her if she thought she could *do* with 'enamelled.' But I was quite taken with my idea— Where is it? I left Annie to settle with this misanthrope, amidst his raw frameworks of the Homes of the Future."

He fumbled with his tablets. "Mats for hall—not to exceed 3s. 9d.... Kerbs ... inquire tiled hearth ... Ah! Here we are: 'Ballade of the Bedroom Suite':—

"Noble the oak you are now displaying,
Subtly the hazel's grainings go,
Walnut's charm there is no gainsaying,
Red as red wine is your rosewood's glow;
Brave and brilliant the ash you show,
Rich your mahogany's hepatite shine,
Cool and sweet your enamel: But oh!

Where are the wardrobes of Painted Pine?"

"They have 'em in the catalogue at five guineas, with a picture—quite as good they are as the more expensive ones. To judge by the picture."

"But that's scarcely the idea you started with," I began.

"Not; it went wrong—ballades often do. The preoccupation of the 'Painted Pine' was too much for me. What's this? 'N.B.— Sludge sells music stools at—' No. Here we are (first half unwritten):—

"White enamelled, like driven snow,
Picked with just one delicate line.
Price you were saying is? Fourteen!—No!
Where are the wardrobes of Painted Pine?"

Comes round again, you see! Then *L'Envoy*:—

"Salesman, sad is the truth I trow:
Winsome walnut can never be mine.
Poets are cheap. And their poetry. So
Where are the wardrobes of Painted Pine?"

"Prosaic! As all true poetry is, nowadays. But, how I tired as the afternoon moved on! At first I was interested in the shopman's amazing lack of imagination, and the glory of that fond dream of mine—love in a cottage, you know—still hung about me. I had ideas come—like that Ballade—and every now and then Annie told me to write notes. I think my last gleam of pleasure was in choosing the drawing-room chairs. There is scope for fantasy in chairs. Then—"

He took some more whisky.

"A kind of grey horror came upon me. I don't know if I can describe it. We went through vast vistas of chairs, of hall-tables, of machine-made pictures, of curtains, huge wildernesses of carpets, and ever this cold, unsympathetic shopman led us on, and ever and again made us buy this or that. He had a perfectly grey eye—the colour of an overcast sky in January—and he seemed neither to hate us nor to detest us, but simply to despise us, to feel such an overwhelming contempt for our petty means and our petty lives, as an archangel might feel for an apple-maggot. It made me think...."

He lit a fresh cigarette.

"I had a kind of vision. I do not know if you will understand. The Warehouse of Life, with our Individual Fate hurrying each of us through. Showing us with a covert sneer all the good things that we cannot afford. A magnificent Rosewood love affair, for instance, deep and rich, fitted complete, some hours of perfect life, some acts of perfect self-sacrifice, perfect self-devotion.... You ask the price."

He shrugged his shoulders.

"Where are the wardrobes of Painted Pine?" I quoted.

"That's it. All the things one might do, if the purse of one's courage were not so shallow. If it wasn't for the lack of that coinage, Bellows, every man might be magnificent. There's heroism, there's such nobility as no one has ever attained to, ready to hand. Anyone, if it were not for this lack of means, might be a human god in twenty-four hours.... You see the article. You cannot buy it. No one buys it. It stands in the emporium, I suppose, for show—on the chance of a million-naire. And the shopman waves his hand to it on your way to the Painted Pine.

"Then you meet other couples and solitary people going about, each with a gloomy salesman leading. The run of them look uncomfortable; some are hot about the ears and in the spiteful phase of ill-temper; all look sick of the business except the raw new-comers. It's the only time they will ever select any furniture, their first chance and their last. Most of their selections are hurried a little. The salesman must not be kept all day.... Yet it goes hard with you if you buy your Object in Life and find it just a 'special line' made to sell.... We're all amateurs at living, just as we are all amateurs at furnishing—or dying. Some of the poor devils one meets carry tattered little scraps of paper, and fumble conscientiously with stumpy pencils. It's a comfort to see how you go, even if you do have to buy rubbish. 'If we have *this* so good, dear, I don't know *how* we shall manage in the kitchen,' says the careful housewife.... So it is we do our shopping in the Great Emporium."

"You will have to rewrite your Ballade," said I, "and put all that in."

"I wish I could," said the poet.

"And while you were having these very fine moods?"

"Annie and the shopman settled most of the furniture between them. Perhaps it's just as well. I was never very good at the practical details of life.... Cigarette's out! Have you any more matches?"

"Horribly depressed you are!" I said.

"There's to-morrow. Well, well...."

And then he went off at a tangent to tell me what he expected to make by his next volume of poems, and so came to the congenial business of running down his contemporaries, and became again the cheerful little Poet that I know.

H. G. Wells

THE LANGUAGE OF FLOWERS

During the early Victorian revival of chivalry the Language of Flowers had some considerable vogue. The Romeo of the mutton-chop whiskers was expected to keep this delicate symbolism in view, and even to display his wit by some dainty conceits in it. An ignorance of the code was fraught with innumerable dangers. A sprig of lilac was a suggestion, a moss-rosebud pushed the matter, was indeed evidence to go to court upon; and unless Charlotte parried with white poplar—a by no means accessible flower—or apricot blossom, or failing these dabbed a cooling dock-leaf at the fellow, he was at her with tulip, heliotrope, and honeysuckle, peach-blossom, white jonquil, and pink, and a really overpowering and suffocating host of attentions. I suppose he got at last to three-cornered notes in the vernacular; and meanwhile what could a poor girl do? There was no downright "No!" in the language of flowers, nothing equivalent to "Go away, please," no flower for "Idiot!" The only possible defence was something in this way: "Your cruelty causes me sorrow," "Your absence is a pleasure." For this, according to the code of Mr. Thomas Miller (third edition, 1841, with elegantly coloured plates) you would have to get a sweet-pea blossom for Pleasure, wormwood for Absence, and indicate Sorrow by the yew, and Cruelty by the stinging-nettle. There is always a little risk of mixing your predicates in this kind of communication, and he might, for instance, read that his Absence caused you Sorrow, but he could scarcely miss the point of the stinging-nettle. That and the gorse carefully concealed were about the only gleams of humour possible in the language. But then it was the appointed tongue of lovers, and while their sickness is upon them they have neither humour nor wit.

This Mr. Thomas Miller wrote abundant flowers of language in his book, and the plates were coloured by hand. By the bye, what a blessed thing colour-printing is! These hand-tinted plates, to an imaginative person, are about as distressing as any plates can very well be. Whenever I look at these triumphs of art over the beauties of nature, with all their weary dabs of crimson, green, blue, and yellow, I think of wretched, anaemic girls fading their youth away in some dismal attic over a publisher's, toiling through the whole edition tint by tint, and being mocked the while by Mr. Miller's alliterative erotics. And they *are* erotics! In one place he writes, "Beautiful art thou, O Broom! on the breezy bosom of the bee-haunted heath"; and throughout he buds and blossoms into similar delights. He wallows in doves and coy toyings and modest blushes, and bowers and meads. He always adds, "Wonderful boy!" to Chatterton's name as if it were a university degree (W.B.), and he invariably refers to Moore as the Bard of Erin, and to Milton as the Bard of Paradise—though Bard of the Bottomless Pit would be more appropriate. However, we are not concerned with Mr. Miller's language so much as with a very fruitful suggestion he throws out, that "it is surely worth while to trace a resemblance between the flower and the emblem it represents" (a turn like that is nothing to Mr. Miller) "which shall at least have some show of reason in it."

Come to think of it, there is something singularly unreasonable about almost all floral symbolism. There is your forget-me-not, pink in the bud, and sapphire in the flower, with a fruit that breaks up into four, the very picture of inconstancy and discursiveness. Yet your lover, with a singular blindness, presents this to his lady when they part. Then the white water-lily is supposed to represent purity of heart, and, mark you, it is white without and its centre is all set about with innumerable golden stamens, while in the middle lies, to quote the words of that distinguished botanist, Mr. Oliver, "a fleshy disc." Could there be a better type of sordid and mercenary deliberation maintaining a fair appearance? The tender apple-blossom, rather than Pretence, is surely a reminder of Eden and the fall of love's devotion into inflated worldliness. The poppy which flaunts its violent colours athwart the bearded corn, and which frets and withers like the Second Mrs. Tanqueray so soon as you bring it to the shelter of a decent home, is made the symbol of Repose. One might almost think Aime Martin and the other great authorities on this subject wrote in a mood of irony.

The daisy, too, presents you Innocence, "companion of the milk-white lamb," Mr. Miller calls it. I am sorry for the milk-white lamb. It was one of the earliest discoveries of systematic botany that the daisy is a fraud, a complicated impostor. *The daisy is not a flower at all.* It is a favourite trap in botanical examinations, a snare for artless young men entering the medical profession. Each of the little yellow things in the centre of the daisy is a flower in itself,—if you look at one with a lens you will find it not unlike a cowslip flower,—and the white rays outside are a great deal more than the petals they ought to be if the Innocence theory is to hold good. There is no such thing as an innocent flower; they are all so many deliberate advertisements to catch the eye of the undecided bee, but any flower almost is simpler than this one. We would make it the emblem of artistic deception, and the confidence trick expert should wear it as his crest.

The violet, again, is a greatly overrated exemplar. It stimulates a certain bashfulness, hangs its head, and passed as modest among our simple grandparents. Its special merit is its perfume, and it pretends to wish to hide that from every eye. But, withal, the fragrance is as far-reaching as any I know. It droops ingenuously. "How *could* you come to me," it seems to say, "when all these really brilliant flowers invite you?" Mere fishing for compliments. All the while it is being sweet, to the very best of its undeniable ability. Then it comes, too, in early spring, without a chaperon, and catches our hearts fresh before they are jaded with the crowded beauties of May. A really modest flower would wait for the other flowers to come first. A subtle affectation is surely a different thing from modesty. The violet is simply artful, the young widow among flowers, and to hold up such a flower as an example is not doing one's duty by the young. For true modesty commend me to the agave, which flowers once only in half a hundred years, as one may see for oneself at the Royal Botanical Gardens.

Enough has been said to show what scope there is for revision of this sentimental Volapuk. Mr. Martin himself scarcely goes so far as I have done, though I have merely worked out his suggestion. His only revolutionary proposal is to displace the wind star by the "rathe primrose" for Forsaken, on the strength of a quotation familiar to every reader of Mason's little text-book on the English language. For the rest he followed his authorities, and has followed them now to the remote recesses of the literary lumber-room and into the twopenny book-box. From that receptacle one copy of him was disinterred only a day or so ago; a hundred and seventy pages of prose, chiefly alliterative, several coloured plates, enthusiastic pencil-marking of a vanished somebody, and, besides, an early Victorian flavour of dust and a dim vision of a silent conversation in a sunlit flower garden—altogether I think very cheap at two-pence. The fashion has changed altogether now. In these days we season our love-making with talk about heredity, philanthropy, and sanitation, and present one another with Fabian publications instead of wild flowers. But in the end, I fancy, the business comes to very much the same thing.

THE LITERARY REGIMEN

At the risk of offending the young beginner's illusions, he must be reminded of one or two homely but important facts bearing upon literary production. Homely as they are, they explain much that is at first puzzling. This perplexing question of distinction; the quality of being somehow *fresh*—individual. Really it is a perfectly simple matter. It is common knowledge that, after a prolonged fast, the brain works in a feeble manner, the current of one's thoughts is pallid and shallow, it is difficult to fix the attention and impossible to mobilise the full forces of the mind. On the other hand, immediately after a sound meal, the brain feels massive, but static. Tea is conducive to a gentle flow of pleasing thoughts, and anyone who has taken Easton's syrup of the hypophosphites will recall at once the state of cerebral erethrism, of general mental alacrity, that followed on a dose. Again, champagne (followed perhaps by a soupçon of whisky) leads to a mood essentially humorous and playful, while about three dozen oysters, taken fasting, will in most cases produce a profound and even ominous melancholy. One might enlarge further upon this topic, on the brutalising influence of beer, the sedative quality of lettuce, the stimulating consequences of curried chicken; but enough has been said to point our argument. It is, that such facts as this can surely indicate only one conclusion, and that is the entire dependence of literary qualities upon the diet of the writer.

I may remind the reader, in confirmation of this suggestion, of what is perhaps the most widely known fact about Carlyle, that on one memorable occasion he threw his breakfast out of the window. Why did he throw his breakfast out of the window? Surely his friends have cherished the story out of no petty love of depreciatory detail? There are, however, those who would have us believe it was mere childish petulance at a chilly rasher or a hard-boiled egg. Such a supposition is absurd. On the other hand, what is more natural than an outburst of righteous indignation at the ruin of some carefully studied climax of feeding? The thoughtful literary beginner who is not altogether submerged in foolish theories of inspiration and natural genius will, we fancy, see pretty clearly that I am developing what is perhaps after all the fundamental secret of literary art.

To come now to more explicit instructions. It is imperative, if you wish to write with any power and freshness at all, that you should utterly ruin your digestion. Any literary person will confirm this statement. At any cost the thing must be done, even if you have to live on German sausage, onions, and cheese to do it. So long as you turn all your dietary to flesh and blood you will get no literature out of it. "We learn in suffering what we teach in song." This is why men who live at home with their mothers, or have their elder sisters to see after them, never, by any chance, however great their literary ambition may be, write anything but minor poetry. They get their meals at regular hours, and done to a turn, and that plays the very devil—if you will pardon the phrase—with one's imagination.

A careful study of the records of literary men in the past, and a considerable knowledge of living authors, suggests two chief ways of losing one's digestion and engendering literary capacity. You go and live in humble lodgings,—we could name dozens of prominent men who have fed a great ambition in this way,—or you marry a nice girl who does not understand housekeeping. The former is the more efficacious method, because, as a rule, the nice girl wants to come and sit on your knee all day, and that is a great impediment to literary composition. Belonging to a club—even a literary club— where you can dine is absolute ruin to the literary beginner. Many a bright young fellow, who has pushed his way, or has been pushed by indiscreet friends, into the society of successful literary men, has been spoilt by this fatal error, and he has saved his stomach to lose his reputation.

Having got rid of your digestion, then, the common condition of all good literature, the next thing is to arrange your dietary for the particular literary effect you desire. And here we may point out the secrecy observed in such matters by literary men. Stevenson fled to Samoa to hide his extremely elaborate methods, and to keep his kitchen servants out of the reach of bribery. Even Sir Walter Besant, though he is fairly communicative to the young aspirant, has dropped no hints of the plain, pure, and wholesome menu he follows. Sala professed to eat everything, but that was probably his badinage. Possibly he had one staple, and took the rest as condiment. Then what did Shakespeare live on? Bacon? And Mr. Barrie, though he has written a delightful book about his pipe and tobacco, full of suggestion to the young humorist, lets out nothing or next to nothing of his meat and drink. His hints about pipes are very extensively followed, and nowadays every ambitious young pressman smokes in public at least one well-burnt briar with an eccentric stem—even at some personal inconvenience. But this jealous reticence on the part of successful men—you notice they never let even the interviewer see their kitchens or the debris of a meal—necessarily throws one back upon rumour and hypothesis in this matter. Mr. Andrew Lang, for instance, is popularly associated with salmon, but that is probably a willful delusion. Excessive salmon, far from engendering geniality, will be found in practice a vague and melancholy diet, tending more towards the magnificent despondency of Mr. Hall Caine.

Nor does Mr. Haggard feed entirely on raw meat. Indeed, for lurid and somewhat pessimistic narrative, there is nothing like the ordinary currant bun, eaten new and in quantity. A light humorous style is best attained by soda-water and dry biscuits, following cafe-noir. The soda-water may be either Scotch or Irish as the taste inclines. For a florid, tawdry style the beginner must take nothing but boiled water, stewed vegetables, and an interest in the movements against vivisection, opium, alcohol, tobacco, sarcophagy, and the male sex.

For contributions to the leading reviews, boiled pork and cabbage may be eaten, with bottled beer, followed by apple dumpling. This effectually suppresses any tendency to facetiousness, or what respectable English people call *double entendre*, and brings you *en rapport* with the serious people who read these publications. So soon as you begin to feel wakeful and restless discontinue writing. For what is vulgarly known as the *fin-de-siecle* type of publication, on the other hand, one should limit oneself to an aerated bread shop for a week or so, with the exception of an occasional tea in a literary household. All people fed mainly on scones become clever. And this regimen, with an occasional debauch upon macaroons, chocolate, and cheap champagne, and brisk daily walks from Oxford Circus, through Regent Street, Piccadilly, and the Green Park, to Westminster and back, should result in an animated society satire.

It is not known what Mr. Kipling takes to make him so peculiar. Many of us would like to know. Possibly it is something he picked up in the jungle—berries or something. A friend who made a few tentative experiments to this end turned out nothing beyond a will, and that he dictated and left incomplete. (It was scarcely on the lines of an ordinary will, being blasphemous, and mentioning no property except his inside.) For short stories of the detective type, strong cold tea and hard biscuits are fruitful eating, while for a social science novel one should take an abundance of boiled rice and toast and water.

However, these remarks are mainly by way of suggestion. Every writer in the end, so soon as his digestion is destroyed, must ascertain for himself the peculiar diet that suits him best—that is, which disagrees with him the most. If everything else fails he might try some chemical food. "Jabber's Food for Authors," by the bye, well advertised, and with portraits of literary men, in their drawing-rooms, "Fed entirely on Jabber's Food," with medical certificates of its unwholesomeness, and favourable and expurgated reviews of works written on it, ought to be a brilliant success among literary aspirants. A small but sufficient quantity of arsenic might with advantage be mixed in.

HOUSE-HUNTING AS AN
OUTDOOR AMUSEMENT

Since Adam and Eve went hand in hand out of the gates of Paradise, the world has travailed under an infinite succession of house-hunts. To-day in every eligible suburb you may see New Adams and New Eves by the score, with rusty keys and pink order-forms in hand, wandering still, in search of the ideal home. To them it is anything but an amusement. Most of these poor pilgrims look simply tired, some are argumentative in addition, but all are disappointed, anxious, and unhappy, their hands dirty with prying among cisterns, and their garments soiled from cellar walls. All, in the exaltation of the wooing days, saw at least the indistinct reflection of the perfect house, but now the Quest is irrevocably in hand they seek and do not find. And such a momentous question it is to them. Are they not choosing the background, the air and the colour, as it were, of the next three or four years, the cardinal years, too! of their lives?

Perhaps the exquisite exasperation of the business for the man who hunts among empty houses for a home is, that it is so entirely a choice of second-hand, or at least ready-made goods. To me, at least, there is a decided suggestion of the dead body in your empty house that has once been occupied. Here, like pale ghosts upon the wall paper, are outlined the pictures of the departed tenant; here are the nails of the invisible curtains, this dent in the wall is all that is sensible of a vanished piano. I could fancy all these things creeping back to visibility as the light grew dim. Someone was irritable in the house, perhaps, and a haunting fragrance of departed quarrels is to be found in the loose door-handles, and the broken bell-pull. Then the blind in the bedroom has a broken string. He was a beer-drinker, for the drip of the tap has left its mark in the cellar; a careless man, for this wall is a record of burst water-pipes; and rough in his methods, as his emendation of the garden gate—a remedy rather worse than the disease—shows. The mark of this prepotent previous man is left on the house from cellar to attic. It is his house really, not mine. And against these haunting individualities set the horrible wholesale flavour, the obvious dexterous builder's economies of a new house. Yet, whatever your repulsion may be, the end is always the same. After you have asked for your ideal house a hundred times or so you begin to see you do not get it. You go the way of your kind. All houses are taken in despair.

But such disgusts as this are for the man who really aims at taking a house. The artist house-hunter knows better than that. He hunts for the hunt's sake, and does not mar his work with a purpose. Then house-hunting becomes a really delight-ful employment, and one strangely neglected in this country. I have heard, indeed, of old ladies who enlivened the intervals of their devotions in this manner, but to the general run of people the thing is unknown. Yet a more entertaining way of spending a half-holiday—having regard to current taste—it should be difficult to imagine. An empty house is realistic literature in the concrete, full of hints and allusions if a little wanting in tangible humanity, and it outdoes the modern story in its own line, by beginning as well as ending in a note of interrogation. That it is not more extensively followed I can only explain by supposing that its merits are generally unsuspected. In which case this book should set a fashion.

One singular thing the house-hunter very speedily discovers is, that the greater portion of the houses in this country are owned by old gentlemen or old ladies who live next door. After a certain age, and especially upon retired tradespeople, house property, either alone or in common with gardening, exercises an irresistible fascination. You always know you are going to meet a landlord or landlady of this type when you read on your order to view, "Key next door but one." Calling next door but one, you are joined after the lapse of a few minutes by a bald, stout gentleman, or a lady of immemorial years, who offers to go over "the property" with you. Apparently the intervals between visits to view are spent in slumber, and these old people come out refreshed and keen to scrutinise their possible new neighbours. They will tell you all about the last tenant, and about the present tenants on either side, and about themselves, and how all the other houses in the neighbourhood are damp, and how they remember when the site of the house was a cornfield, and what they do for their rheumatism. As one hears them giving a most delightful vent to their loquacity, the artistic house-hunter feels all the righteous self-applause of a kindly deed. Sometimes they get extremely friendly. One old gentleman—to whom anyone under forty must have seemed puerile—presented the gentle writer with three fine large green apples as a kind of earnest of his treatment: apples, no doubt, of some little value, since they excited the audible envy of several little boys before they were disposed of.

Sometimes the landlord has even superintended the building of the house himself, and then it often has peculiar distinctions—no coal cellar, or a tower with turrets, or pillars of ornamental marble investing the portico with disproportionate dignity. One old gentleman, young as old gentlemen go, short of stature, of an agreeable red colour, and with short iron-grey hair, had a niche over the front door containing a piece of statuary. It gave one the impression of the Venus of Milo in chocolate pyjamas. "It was nood at first," said the landlord, "but the neighbourhood is hardly educated up to art, and objected. So I gave it that brown paint."

On one expedition the artistic house-hunter was accompanied by Euphemia. Then it was he found Hill Crest, a vast edifice at the incredible rent of L40 a year, with which a Megatherial key was identified. It took the two of them, not to mention an umbrella, to turn this key. The rent was a mystery, and while they were in the house—a thunderstorm kept them there some time—they tried to imagine the murder. From the top windows they could see the roofs of the opposite houses in plan.

"I wonder how long it would take to get to the top of the house from the bottom?" said Euphemia.

"Certainly longer than we could manage every day," said the artistic house-hunter. "Fancy looking for my pipe in all these rooms. Starting from the top bedroom at the usual time, I suppose one would arrive downstairs to breakfast about eleven, and then we should have to be getting upstairs again by eight o'clock if we wanted any night's rest worth having. Or we might double or treble existence, live a Gargantuan life to match the house, make our day of forty-eight hours instead of twenty-four. By doubling everything we should not notice the hole it made in our time getting about the place. Perhaps by making dinner last twice as long, eating twice as much, and doing everything on the scale of two to one, we might adapt ourselves to our environment in time, grow twice as big."

"*Then* we might be very comfortable here," said Euphemia.

They went downstairs again. By that time it was thundering and raining heavily. The rooms were dark and gloomy. The big side door, which would not shut unless locked from the outside, swayed and banged as the gusts of wind swept round the house. But they had a good time in the front kitchen, playing cricket with an umbrella and the agent's order crumpled into a ball. Presently the artistic house-hunter lifted Euphemia on to the tall dresser, and they sat there swinging their feet patiently until the storm should leave off and release them.

"I should feel in this kitchen," said Euphemia, "like one of my little dolls must have felt in the dolls'-house kitchen I had once. The top of her head just reached the level of the table. There were only four plates on the dresser, but each was about half her height across—"

"Your reminiscences are always entertaining," said the artistic house-hunter; "still they fail to explain the absorbing mystery of this house being to let at L40 a year." The problem raised his curiosity, but though he made inquiries he found no reason for the remarkably low rent or the continued emptiness of the house. It was a specimen puzzle for the house-hunter. A large house with a garden of about half an acre, and with accommodation for about six families, going begging for L40 a year. Would it let at eighty? Some such problem, however, turns up in every house-hunt, and it is these surprises that give the sport its particular interest and delight. Always provided the mind is not unsettled by any ulterior notion of settling down.

OF BLADES AND BLADERY

The Blade is not so much a culture as a temperament, and Bladery—if the thing may have the name—a code of sentiments rather than a ritual. It is the rococo school of behaviour, the flamboyant gentleman, the gargoyle life. The Blade is the tribute innocence pays to vice. He may look like a devil and belong to a church. And the clothing of the Blade, being symbolical, is a very important part of him. It must show not only a certain tastiness, but also decision in the accent, courage in the pattern, and a Dudley Hardihood of outline. A Blade must needs take the colour of his social standing, but all Blades have the same essential qualities. And all Blades have this quality, that they despise and contemn other Blades from the top downward. (But where the bottommost Blade comes no man can tell.)

A well-bred Blade—though he be a duke—tends to wear his hat tilted a little over the right eyebrow, and a piece of hair is pulled coquettishly down just below the brim. His collar is high, and a very large bow is worn slightly askew. This may be either cream-coloured or deep blue, with spots of white, or it may be red, or buff, but not green, because of badinage. The Blade of the middle class displays a fine gold watch-chain, and his jacket and vest may be of a rough black cloth or blue serge. The trousering may be of a suit with the jacket, or tasteful, and the shoes must be long. The betting man, adorned, is a perfect Blade. There is often a large and ornamental stick, which is invariably carried head downwards. And note, that the born Blade instinctively avoids any narrowness of pose. In walking he thrusts out his shoulders, elbows, and knees, and it is rather the thing to dominate a sphere of influence beyond this by swinging his stick. At first the beginner will find this weapon a little apt to slip from the hand and cause inconvenience to the general public; but he must not mind that. After a few such misadventures he will acquire dexterity.

All Blades smoke—publicly at least. To smoke a white meerschaum in the streets, however, is very inferior form. The proper smoking is a briar, and, remember, it is not smart to have a new pipe. So soon as he buys it, the Blade takes his pipe home, puts it on a glowing fire to burn the rim, scrapes this away, burns it again, and so on until it looks a sullen desperado of a pipe—a pipe with a wild past. Sometimes he cannot smoke a pipe. In this case he may—for his stomach's sake— smoke a cigarette. And, besides, there is something cynical about a cigarette. For the very young Blade there are certain makes of cigarette that burn well—they are mixed with nitre— and these may be smoked by holding them in the left hand and idly swinging them to and fro in the air. If it were not for the public want of charity, I would recommend a well-known brand. A Blade may always escape a cigar by feigning a fastidious taste. "None of your Cabanas" is rather good style.

The Blade, it must be understood—especially by the Blade's friends—spends his time in a whirl of dissipation. That is the symbolism of the emphatic obliquity of the costume. First, he drinks. The Blade at Harrow, according to a reliable authority, drinks cherry brandy and even champagne; other Blades consume whisky-and-soda; the less costly kind of Blade does it on beer. And here the beginner is often at a loss. Let us say he has looked up the street and down, ascertained that there are no aunts in the air, and then plunged into his first public-house. How shall he ask for his liquor? "I will take a glass of ale, if you please, Miss," seems tame for a Blade. It may be useful to know a more suitable formula. Just at present, we may assure the Blade neophyte, it is all the rage to ask for "Two of swipes, ducky." Go in boldly, bang down your money as loudly as possible, and shout that out at the top of your voice. If it is a barman, though, you had better not say "ducky." The slang will, we can assure him, prove extremely effective.

Then the Blade gambles; but over the gambling of the Blade it is well to draw a veil—a partially translucent and coquettish veil, through which we can see the thing dimly, and enhanced in its enormity. You must patronise the Turf, of course, and have money on horses, or you are no Blade at all, but a mere stick. The Harrow Blade has his book on all the big races in the calendar; and the great and noble game of Nap—are not Blades its worshippers wherever the sun shines and a pack of cards is obtainable? Baccarat, too. Many a glorious Blade has lost his whole term's pocket-money at a single sitting at that noble game. And the conversation of the Blade must always be brilliant in the extreme, like the flashing of steel in the sunlight. It is usually cynical and worldly, sometimes horrible enough to make a governess shudder, but always epigrammatic. Epigrams and neat comparisons are much easier to make than is vulgarly supposed. "Schoolmasters hang about the crops of knowledge like dead crows about a field, examples and warnings to greedy souls." "Marriage is the beginning of philosophy, and the end is, 'Do not marry.'" "All women are constant, but some discover mistakes." "One is generally repentant when one is found out, and remorseful when one can't do it again." A little practice, and this kind of thing may be ground out almost without thinking. Occasionally, in your conversation with ladies, you may let an oath slip. (Better not let your aunt hear you.) Apologise humbly at once, of course. But it will give them a glimpse of the lurid splendour of your private life.

And that brings us to the central thing of the Blade's life, the eternal Feminine! Pity them, be a little sorry for them—the poor souls cannot be Blades. They must e'en sit and palpitate while the Blade flashes. The accomplished Blade goes through life looking unspeakable wickedness at everything feminine he meets, old and young, rich and poor, one with another. He reeks with intrigue. Every Blade has his secrets and mysteries in this matter—remorse even for crimes. You do not know all that his handsome face may hide. Even he does not know. He may have sat on piers and talked to shop-girls, kissed house-maids, taken barmaids to music halls, conversed with painted wickedness in public places—nothing is too much for him. And oh! the reckless protestations of love he has made, the broken promises, the broken hearts! Yet men must be Blades, though women may weep; and every Blade must take his barmaid to a music hall at least once, even if she be taller than himself. Until then his manhood is not assured.

Just one hint in conclusion. A Blade who collects stamps, or keeps tame rabbits, or eats sweets, oranges, or apples in the streets, or calls names publicly after his friends, is no Blade at all, but a boy still. So, with our blessing, he swaggers on his way and is gone. A Don Juan as fresh as spring, a rosebud desperado. May he never come upon just cause for repentance!

H. G. Wells

OF CLEVERNESS

APROPOS OF ONE CRICHTON

Crichton is an extremely clever person—abnormally, indeed almost unnaturally, so. He is not merely clever at this or that, but clever all round; he gives you no consolations. He goes about being needlessly brilliant. He caps your jests and corrects your mistakes, and does your special things over again in newer and smarter ways. Any really well-bred man who presumed so far would at least be plain or physically feeble, or unhappily married by way of apology, but the idea of so much civility seems never to have entered Crichton's head. He will come into a room where we are jesting perhaps, and immediately begin to flourish about less funny perhaps but decidedly more brilliant jests, until at last we retire one by one from the conversation and watch him with savage, weary eyes over our pipes. He invariably beats me at chess, invariably. People talk about him and ask my opinion of him, and if I venture to criticise him they begin to look as though they thought I was jealous. Grossly favourable notices of his books and his pictures crop up in the most unlikely places; indeed I have almost given up newspapers on account of him. Yet, after all—

This cleverness is not everything. It never pleases me, and I doubt sometimes if it pleases anyone. Suppose you let off some clever little thing, a subtlety of expression, a paradox, an allusive suggestive picture; how does it affect ordinary people? Those who are less clever than yourself, the unspecialised, unsophisticated average people, are simply annoyed by the puzzle you set them; those who are cleverer find your cleverness mere obvious stupidity; and your equals, your competitors in cleverness, are naturally your deadly rivals. The fact is this cleverness, after all, is merely egotism in its worst and unwisest phase. It is an incontinence of brilliance, graceless and aggressive, a glaring swagger. The drunken helot of cleverness is the creature who goes about making puns. A mere step above comes the epigram, the isolated epigram framed and glazed. Then such impressionist art as Crichton's pictures, mere puns in paint. What they mean is nothing, they arrest a quiet decent-minded man like myself with the same spasmodic disgust as a pun in literature—the subject is a transparent excuse; they are mere indecent and unedifying exhibitions of himself. He thinks it is something superlative to do everything in a startling way. He cannot even sign his name without being offensive. He lacks altogether the fundamental quality of a gentleman, the magnanimity to be commonplace. I—

On the score of personal dignity, why should a young man of respectable antecedents and some natural capacity stoop to this kind of thing? To be clever is the last desperate resort of the feeble, it is the merit of the ambitious slave. You cannot conquer *vi et armis*, you cannot stomach a decent inferiority, so you resort to lively, eccentric, and brain-wearying brilliance to ingratiate yourself. The cleverest animal by far is the monkey, and compare that creature's undignified activity with the mountainous majesty of the elephant!

And I cannot help thinking, too, that cleverness must be the greatest obstacle a man can possibly have in his way upward in the world. One never sees really clever people in positions of trust, never widely influential or deeply rooted. Look, for instance, at the Royal Academy, at the Judges, at—But there! The very idea of cleverness is an all-round readiness and looseness that is the very negation of stability.

Whenever Crichton has been particularly exasperating, getting himself appreciated in a new quarter, or rising above his former successes, I find some consolation in thinking of my

Uncle Augustus. He was the glory of our family. Even Aunt Charlotte's voice drooped a little in the mention of his name. He was conspicuous for an imposing and even colossal stupidity: he rose to eminence through it, and, what is more, to wealth and influence. He was as reliable, as unlikely to alter his precise position, or do anything unexpected, as the Pyramids of Egypt. I do not know any topic upon which he was not absolutely uninformed, and his contributions to conversation, delivered in that ringing baritone of his, were appallingly dull. Often I have seen him utterly flatten some cheerful clever person of the Crichton type with one of his simple garden-roller remarks—plain, solid, and heavy, which there was no possibility either of meeting or avoiding. He was very successful in argument, and yet he never fenced. He simply came down. It was, so to speak, a case of small sword *versus* the avalanche. His moral inertia was tremendous. He was never excited, never anxious, never jaded; he was simply massive. Cleverness broke upon him like shipping on an ironbound coast. His monument is like him—a plain large obelisk of coarse granite, unpretending in its simple ugliness and prominent a mile off. Among the innumerable little white sorrows of the cemetery it looks exactly as he used to look among clever people.

Depend upon it cleverness is the antithesis of greatness. The British Empire, like the Roman, was built up by dull men. It may be we shall be ruined by clever ones. Imagine a regiment of lively and eccentric privates! There never was a statesman yet who had not some ballast of stupidity, and it seems to me that part at least of the essentials of a genius is a certain divine dulness. The people we used to call the masters—Shakespeare, Raphael, Milton, and so forth—had a certain simplicity Crichton lacks. They do not scintillate nearly so much as he does, and they do not give that same uncomfortable feeling of internal strain. Even Homer nods. There are restful places in their work, broad meadows of breezy flatness, calms. But Crichton has no Pacific Ocean to mitigate his everlasting weary passage of Cape Horn: it is all point and prominence, point and prominence.

No doubt this Crichton is having a certain vogue now, but it cannot last. I wish him no evil, of course, but I cannot help thinking he will presently have had his day. This epoch of cleverness must be very near its last flare. The last and the abiding thought of humanity is peace. A dull man will presently be sought like the shadow of a great rock in a thirsty land. Dulness will be the New Genius. "Give us dull books," people will cry, "great dull restful pictures. We are weary, very weary." This hectic, restless, incessant phase in which we travail—*fin-de-siecle*, "decadent," and all the rest of it—will pass away. A chubby, sleepy literature, large in aim, colossal in execution, rotund and tranquil will lift its head. And this Crichton will become a classic, Messrs. Mudie will sell surplus copies of his works at a reduction, and I shall cease to be worried by his disgusting success.

THE POSE NOVEL

I watched the little spurts of flame jet out from between the writhing pages of my manuscript, watched the sheets coil up in their fiery anguish and start one from another. I helped the fire to the very vitals of the mass by poking the brittle heap, and at last the sacrifice was over, the flames turned from pink to blue and died out, the red glow gave place to black, little luminous red streaks coiled across the charred sheets and vanished at the margins, and only the ashes of my inspiration remained. The ink was a lustrous black on the dull blackness of the burnt paper. I could still read this much of my indiscretion remaining, "He smiled at them all and said nothing."

"Fool!" I said, and stirred the crackling mass into a featureless heap of black scraps. Then with my chin on my fists and elbows on knees I stared at the end of my labours.

I suppose, after all, there has been some profit out of the thing. Satan finds some mischief still for idle hands to do, and one may well thank Heaven it was only a novel. Still, it means many days out of my life, and I would be glad to find some positive benefit accruing. Clearly, in the first place, I have eased my mind of some execrable English. I am cleaner now by some dozen faulty phrases that I committed and saw afterwards in all the nakedness of typewriting. (Thank Heaven for typewriting! Were it not for that, this thing had gone to the scoffing of some publisher's reader, and another had known my shame.) And I shall not write another pose novel.

I am inclined to think these pose novels the wild oats of authorship. We sit down in the heyday of our youth to write the masterpiece. Obviously, it must be a novel about a man and a woman, and something as splendid as we can conceive of in that way. We look about us. We do not go far for perfection. One of the brace holds the pen and the other is inside his or her head; and so Off! to the willing pen. Only a few years ago we went slashing among the poppies with a walking-stick, and were, we said boldly and openly, Harolds and Hectors slaying our thousands. Now of course we are grown up to self-respect, and must needs be a little disingenuous about it. But as the story unfolds there is no mistaking the likeness, in spite of the transfiguration. This bold, decided man who performs such deeds of derring-do in the noisome slum, knocks down the burly wife-beater, rescues an unmistakable Miss Clapton from the knife of a Lascar, and is all the while cultivating a virtuous consumption that stretches him on an edifying, pathetic, and altogether beautiful deathbed in the last chapter—My dear Authorling, cry my friends, we hear the squeak of that little voice of yours in every word he utters. Is *that* what you aspire to be, that twopence-coloured edition of yourself? Heaven defend you from your desires!

Yet there was a singular fascination in writing the book; to be in anticipation my own sympathetic historian, to joy with my joys yet to come, and sorrow with my sorrows, to bear disaster like a man, and at last to close my own dear eyes, and with a swelling heart write my own epitaph. The pleasure remained with me until I reached the end. How admirably I strutted in front of myself! And I and the better self of me that was flourishing about in the book—we pretended not to know each other for what we were. He was myself with a wig and a sham visiting card, and I owed it to myself to respect my disguise. I made him with very red hair—my hair is fairly dark—and shifted his university from London to Cambridge. Clearly it could not be the same person, I argued. But I endowed him with all the treasures of myself; I made him say all the good things I might have said had I thought of them opportunely, and all the noble thoughts that occurred to me afterwards occurred to him at the time. He was myself—myself at a premium, myself without any drawbacks, the quintessence and culmination of me. And yet somehow when he came back from the typewriter he seemed a bit of an ass.

Probably every tadpole author writes a pose novel—at least I hope so for the sake of my self-respect. Most, after my fashion, burn the thing, or benevolent publishers lose it. It is an ill thing if by some accident the tadpole tale survives the tadpole stage. The authoress does the feminine equivalent, but I should judge either that she did it more abundantly or else that she burned less. Has she never swept past you with a scornful look, disdained you in all the pride of her beauty, rippled laughter at you, or amazed you with her artless girlishness? And even after the early stages some of the trick may survive, unless I read books with malice instead of charity. I must confess, though, that I have a weakness for finding mine author among his puppets. I conceive him always taking the best parts, like an actor-manager or a little boy playing with his sisters. I do not read many novels with sincere belief, and I like to get such entertainment from them as I can. So that these artless little self-revelations are very sweet and precious to me among all the lay figures, tragedy and comedy. Since the deception is transparent I make the most of the transparency, and love to see the clumsy fingers on the strings of the marionettes. And this will be none the less pleasant now that I have so narrowly escaped giving this entertainment to others.

I suppose this stage is a necessary one. We begin with ignorance and the imagination, the material of the pose novel. Later come self-knowledge, disappointments and self-consciousness, and the prodigals of fiction stay themselves upon the husks of epigram and cynicism, and in the place of artless aspiration are indeed in plain black and white very desperate characters. It is after all only another pose—the pose of not posing. We, the common clay of the world of letters, must needs write in this way, because we cannot forget our foolish little selves in our work. But some few there are who sit as gods above their private universes, and write without passion or vanity. At least, so I have been told. These be the true artists of letters, the white windows upon the truth of things. We by comparison are but stained glass in our own honour, and do but obstruct the view with our halos and attitudes. Yet even Shakespeare, the critics tell us—and they say they know—posed in the character of Hamlet.

After all, the pose novel method has at times attained to the level of literature. Charlotte Bronte might possibly have found no other topic had she disdained the plain little woman with a shrewish tongue; and where had Charles Kingsley been if the vision of a curate rampant had not rejoiced his heart? Still, I am not sorry that this novel is burned. Even now it was ridiculous, and the time might have come when this book, full of high, if foolish aims, and the vain vast promise of well-meaning youth, had been too keen a reproach to be endured. Three volumes of good intentions! It is too much. There was more than a novel burning just now. After this I shall be in a position to take a humorist's view of life.

H. G. Wells

THE VETERAN CRICKETER

My old cricketer was seized, he says, some score of years ago now, by sciatica, clutched indeed about the loins thereby, and forcibly withdrawn from the practice of the art; since when a certain predisposition to a corpulent habit has lacked its natural check of exercise, and a broadness almost Dutch has won upon him. Were it not for this, which renders his contours and his receding aspect unseemly, he would be indeed a venerable-looking person, having a profile worthy of a patriarch, tinged though it may be with an unpatriarchal jollity, and a close curly beard like that of King David. He lives by himself in a small cottage outside the village—hating women with an unaccountable detestation—and apparently earns a precarious livelihood, and certainly the sincere aversion of the country side, by umpiring in matches, and playing whist and "Nap" with such as will not be so discreet and economical as to bow before his superior merit.

His neighbours do not like him, because he will not take their cricket or their whist seriously, because he will persist in offering counsel and the stimulus of his gift of satire. All whist than his he avers is "Bumble-puppy." His umpiring is pedagogic in tone; he fails to see the contest in the game. To him, who has heard his thousands roar as the bails of the best of All England went spinning, these village matches are mere puerile exercises to be corrected. His corrections, too, are Olympian, done, as it were, in red ink, vivid, and without respect of persons. Particularly he gibes. He never uses vulgar bad language himself, but has a singular power of engendering it in others. He has a word "gaby," which he will sometimes enlarge to "stuppid gaby," the which, flung neatly into a man who has just missed a catch, will fill the same with a whirl of furious curses difficult to restrain. And if perchance one should escape, my ancient cricketer will be as startled as Cadmus at the crop he has sown. And not only startled but pained at human wickedness and the follies of a new generation. "Why can't you play without swearing, Muster Gibbs?" he will say, catching the whispered hope twenty yards away, and proclaiming it to a censorious world. And so Gibbs, our grocer and draper, and one made much of by the vicar, is shamed before the whole parish, and damned even as he desired.

To our vicar, a well-meaning, earnest, and extremely nervous man, he displays a methodical antagonism. Our vicar is the worst of all possible rural vicars—unripe, a glaring modern, no classical scholar, no lover of nature, offensively young and yet not youthful, an indecent politician. He was meant to labour amid Urban Myriads, to deal with Social Evils, Home Rule, the Woman Question, and the Reunion of Christendom, attend Conferences and go with the *Weltgeist*—damn him!— wherever the *Weltgeist* is going. He presents you jerkily—a tall lean man of ascetic visage and ample garments, a soul clothed not so much in a fleshy body as in black flaps that ever trail behind its energy. Where they made him Heaven knows. No university owns him. It may be he is a renegade Dissenting minister, neither good Church nor wholesome Noncon- formity. Him my cricketer regards with malignant respect. Respect he shows by a punctilious touching of his hat brim, directed to the sacred office; all the rest is malignity, and aimed at the man that fills it. They come into contact on the cricket- field, and on the committee of our reading-room. For our vicar, in spite of a tendency to myopia, conceives it his duty to encourage cricket by his participation. *Duty*—to encourage cricket! So figure the scene to yourself. The sunlit green, and a match in progress,—the ball has just snipped a stump askew,—my ancient, leaning on a stout cabbage stick, and with the light overcoat that is sacred to umpires upon his arm.

"*Out*, Billy Durgan," says he, and adds, *ex cathedra*, "and one you ought to ha' hit for four."

Then appears our vicar in semi-canonicals, worn "to keep up his position," or some such folly, nervous about the adjustment of his hat and his eyeglasses. He approaches the pitch, smiling the while to show his purely genial import and to anticipate and explain any amateurish touches. He reaches the wicket and poses himself, as the convenient book he has studied directs. "You'll be caught, Muster Shackleforth, if you keep your shoulder up like that," says the umpire. "Ya-a-ps! that's worse!"—forgetting himself in his zeal for attitude. And then a voice cries "Play!"

The vicar swipes wildly, cuts the ball for two, and returns to his wicket breathless but triumphant. Next comes a bye, and then over. The misguided cleric, ever pursuing a theory of foolish condescension to his betters at the game, and to show there is no offence at the "Yaaps," takes the opportunity, although panting, of asking my ancient if his chicks—late threatened with staggers—are doing well. What would he think if my cricketer retaliated by asking, in the pause before the sermon, how the vicarage pony took his last bolus? The two men do not understand one another. My cricketer waves the hens aside, and revenges himself, touching his hat at intervals, by some offensively obvious remarks—as to a mere beginner—about playing with a straight bat. And the field sniggers none too furtively. I sympathise with his malice. Cricket is an altogether too sacred thing to him to be tampered with on merely religious grounds. However, our vicar gets himself caught at the first opportunity, and so being removed from my veteran's immediate environment, to their common satisfaction, the due ritual of the great game is resumed.

My ancient cricketer abounds in reminiscence of the glorious days that have gone for ever. He can still recall the last echoes of the "throwing" controversy that agitated Nyren, when over-arm bowling began, and though he never played himself in a beaver hat, he can, he says, recollect seeing matches so played.

In those days everyone wore tall hats—the policeman, the milkman, workmen of all sorts. Some people I fancy must have bathed in them and gone to bed wearing them. He recalls the Titans of that and the previous age, and particularly delights in the legend of Noah Mann, who held it a light thing to walk twenty miles from Northchapel to Hambledon to practise every Tuesday afternoon, and wander back after dark. He himself as a stripling would run a matter of four miles, after a day's work in the garden where he was employed, to attend an hour's practice over the downs before the twilight made the balls invisible. And afterwards came Teutonic revelry or wanderings under the summer starlight, as the mood might take him. For there was a vein of silent poetry in the youth of this man.

He hates your modern billiard-table pitch, and a batting of dexterous snickery. He likes "character" in a game, gigantic hitting forward, bowler-planned leg catches, a cunning obliquity in a wicket that would send the balls mysteriously askew. But dramatic breaks are now a thing unknown in trade cricket. One legend of his I doubt; he avers that once at Brighton, in a match between Surrey and Sussex, he saw seven wickets bowled by some such aid in two successive overs. I have never been able to verify this. I believe that, as a matter of fact, the thing has never occurred, but he tells it often in a fine crescendo of surprise, and the refrain, "Out HE came." His first beginning is a cheerful anecdote of a crew of "young gentlemen" from Cambridge staying at the big house, and a challenge to the rustic talent of "me and Billy Hall," who "played a bit at that time," "of me and Billy Hall" winning the pitch and going in first, of a memorable if uncivil stand at the wickets through a long hot afternoon, and a number of young gentlemen from Cambridge painfully discovering local talent by exhaustive fielding in the park, a duty they honourably discharged.

I am fond of my old cricketer, in spite of a certain mendacious and malign element in him. His yarns of gallant stands and unexpected turns of fortune, of memorable hits and eccentric umpiring, albeit tending sometimes incredibly to his glory, are full of the flavour of days well spent, of bright mornings of play, sunlit sprawlings beside the score tent, warmth, the flavour of bitten grass stems, and the odour of crushed turf. One seems to hear the clapping hands of village ancients, and their ululations of delight. One thinks of stone jars with cool drink swishing therein, of shouting victories and memorable defeats, of eleven men in a drag, and tuneful and altogether glorious home-comings by the light of the moon. His were the Olympian days of the sport, when noble squires were its patrons, and every village a home and nursery of stalwart cricketers, before the epoch of special trains, gate-money, star elevens, and the tumultuous gathering of idle cads to jabber at a game they cannot play.

CONCERNING A CERTAIN LADY

This lady wears a blue serge suit and a black hat, without flippancy; she is a powerfully built lady and generally more or less flushed, and she is aunt, apparently, to a great number of objectionable-looking people. I go in terror of her. Yet the worm will turn at last, and so will the mild, pacific literary man. Her last outrage was too much even for my patience. It was committed at Gloucester Road Station the other afternoon. I was about to get into a train for Wimbledon,— and there are only two of them to the hour,—and, so far as I could see, the whole world was at peace with me. I felt perfectly secure. The aegis of the *pax Britannica*—if you will pardon the expression—was over me. For the moment the thought of the lady in the blue serge was quite out of my mind. I had just bought a newspaper, and had my hand on the carriage door. The guard was fluttering his flag.

Then suddenly she swooped out of space, out of the infinite unknown, and hit me. She always hits me when she comes near me, and I infer she hits everyone she comes across. She hit me this time in the chest with her elbow and knocked me away from the door-handle. She hit me very hard; indeed, she was as fierce as I have ever known her. With her there were two nieces and a nephew, and the nephew hit me too. He was a horrid little boy in an Eton suit of the kind that they do not wear at Eton, and he hit me with his head and pushed at me with his little pink hands. The nieces might have been about twenty-two and thirteen respectively, and I infer that they were apprenticed to her. All four people seemed madly excited. "It's

H. G. Wells

just starting!" they screamed, and the train was, indeed, slowly moving. Their object—so far as they had an object and were not animated by mere fury—appeared to be to assault me and then escape in the train. The lady in blue got in and then came backwards out again, sweeping the smaller girl behind her upon the two others, who were engaged in hustling me. "It's 'smoking!'" she cried. I could have told her that, if she had asked instead of hitting me. The elder girl, by backing dexterously upon me, knocked my umbrella out of my hand, and when I stooped to pick it up the little boy knocked my hat off. I will confess they demoralised me with their archaic violence. I had some thought of joining in their wild amuck, whooping, kicking out madly, perhaps assaulting a porter,—I think the lady in blue would have been surprised to find what an effective addition to her staff she had picked up,—but before I could collect my thoughts sufficiently to do any definite thing the whole affair was over. A porter was slamming doors on them, the train was running fast out of the station, and I was left alone with an unmannerly newsboy and an unmannerly porter on the platform. I waited until the porter was out of the way, and then I hit the newsboy for laughing at me, but even with that altercation it was a tedious wait for the next train to Wimbledon.

This is the latest of my encounters with this lady, but it has decided me to keep silence no longer. She has been persecuting me now for years in all parts of London. It may be I am her only victim, but, on the other hand, she may be in the habit of annoying the entire class of slender and inoffensive young men. If so, and they will communicate with me through the publishers of this little volume, we might do something towards suppressing her, found an Anti-Energetic-Lady-League, or something of that sort. For if there was ever a crying wrong that clamoured for suppression it is this violent woman.

She is, even now, flagrantly illegal. She might be given in charge for hitting people at any time, and be warned, or fined, or given a week. But somehow it is only when she is overpast and I am recovering my wits that I recollect that she might be dealt with in this way. She is the chartered libertine of British matrons, and assaulteth where she listeth. The blows I have endured from her? She fights people who are getting into 'buses. It is no mere accidental jostling, but a deliberate shouldering, poking with umbrellas, and clawing. It is her delight to go to the Regent Circus corner of Piccadilly, about half-past seven in the evening, accompanied by a genteel rout of daughters, and fill up whole omnibuses with them. At that hour there are work-girls and tired clerks, and the like worn-out anaemic humanity trying to get home for an hour or so of rest before bed, and they crowd round the 'buses very eagerly. They are little able to cope with her exuberant vitality, being ill-nourished and tired from the day's work, and she simply mows through them and fills up every vacant place they covet before their eyes. Then, I can never count change even when my mind is tranquil, and she knows that, and swoops threateningly upon me in booking offices and stationers' shops. When I am dodging cabs at crossings she will appear from behind an omnibus or carriage and butt into me furiously. She holds her umbrella in her folded arms just as the Punch puppet does his staff, and with as deadly effect. Sometimes she discards her customary navy blue and puts on a glittering bonnet with bead trimmings, and goes and hurts people who are waiting to enter the pit at theatres, and especially to hurt me. She is fond of public shows, because they afford such possibilities of hurting me. Once I saw her standing partly on a seat and partly on another lady in the church of St. George's, Hanover Square, partly, indeed, watching a bride cry, but chiefly, I expect, scheming how she could get round to me and hurt me. Then there was an occasion at the Academy when she was peculiarly aggressive. I was sitting next my lame friend when she marked me. Of course she came at once and sat right upon us. "Come along, Jane," I heard her say, as I struggled to draw my flattened remains from under her; "this gentleman will make room."

My friend was not so entangled and had escaped on the other side. She noticed his walk. "Oh, don't *you* get up," she said.

"*This* gentleman," she indicated my convulsive struggles to free myself, "will do that. *I did not see that you were a cripple.*"

It may be some of my readers will recognise the lady now. It can be—for the honour of womankind—only one woman. She is an atavism, a survival of the age of violence, a Palaeolithic squaw in petticoats. I do not know her name and address or I would publish it. I do not care if she kills me the next time she meets me, for the limits of endurance have been passed. If she kills me I shall die a martyr in the cause of the Queen's peace. And if it is only one woman, then it was the same lady, more than half intoxicated, that I saw in the Whitechapel Road cruelly ill-treating a little costermonger. If it was not she it was certainly her sister, and I do not care who knows it.

What to do with her I do not know. A League, after all, seems ineffectual; she would break up any League. I have thought of giving her in charge for assault, but I shrink from the invidious publicity of that. Still, I am in grim earnest to do something. I think at times that the compulsory adoption of a narrow doorway for churches and places of public entertainment might be some protection for quiet, inoffensive people. How she would rage outside to be sure! Yet that seems a great undertaking.

But this little paper is not so much a plan of campaign as a preliminary defiance. Life is a doubtful boon while one is never safe from assault, from hitting and shoving, from poking with umbrellas, being sat upon, and used as a target for projectile nephews and nieces. I warn her—possibly with a certain quaver in my voice—that I am in revolt. If she hits me again— I will not say the precise thing I will do, but I warn her, very solemnly and deliberately, that she had better not hit me again.

And so for the present the matter remains.

THE SHOPMAN

If I were really opulent, I would not go into a shop at all—I would have a private secretary. If I were really determined, Euphemia would do these things. As it is, I find buying things in a shop the most exasperating of all the many trying duties of life. I am sometimes almost tempted to declare myself Adamite to escape it. The way the shopman eyes you as you enter his den, the very spread of his fingers, irritate me. "What can I have the pleasure?" he says, bowing forward at me, and with his eye on my chin—and so waits.

Now I hate incomplete sentences, and confound his pleasure! I don't go into a shop to give a shopman pleasure. But your ordinary shopman must needs pretend you delight and amuse him. I say, trying to display my dislike as plainly as possible, "Gloves." "Gloves, yessir," he says. Why should he? I suppose he thinks I require to be confirmed in my persuasion that I want gloves. "Calf—kid—dogskin?" How should *I* know the technicalities of his traffic? "Ordinary gloves," I say, disdaining his petty distinctions. "About what price, sir?" he asks.

Now that always maddens me. Why should I be expected to know the price of gloves? I'm not a commercial traveller nor a wholesale dealer, and I don't look like one. Neither am I constitutionally parsimonious nor petty. I am a literary man, unworldly, and I wear long hair and a soft hat and a peculiar overcoat to indicate the same to ordinary people. Why, I say, should I know the price of gloves? I know they are some ordinary price—elevenpence-halfpenny, or three-and-six, or

H. G. Wells

seven-and-six, or something—one of those prices that every-thing is sold at—but further I don't go. Perhaps I say elevenpence-halfpenny at a venture.

His face lights up with quiet malice. "Don't keep them, sir," he says. I can tell by his expression that I am ridiculously low, and so being snubbed. I think of trying with three-and-six, or seven-and-six; the only other probable prices for things that I know, except a guinea and five pounds. Then I see the absurdity of the business, and my anger comes surging up.

"Look here!" I say, as bitterly as possible. "I don't come here to play at Guessing Games. Never mind your prices. I want some gloves. Get me some!"

This cows him a little, but very little. "May I ask your size, sir?" he says, a trifle more respectfully.

One would think I spent all my time remembering the size of my gloves. However, it is no good resenting it. "It's either seven or nine," I say in a tired way.

He just begins another question, and then he catches my eye and stops and goes away to obtain some gloves, and I get a breathing space. But why do they keep on with this cross-examination? If I knew exactly what I wanted—description, price, size—I should not go to a shop at all, it would save me such a lot of trouble just to send a cheque to the Stores. The only reason why I go into a tradesman's shop is because I don't know what I want exactly, am in doubt about the name or the size, or the price, or the fashion, and want a specialist to help me. The only reason for having shopmen instead of automatic machines is that one requires help in buying things. When I want gloves, the shopman ought to understand his business sufficiently well to know better than I do what particular kind of gloves I ought to be wearing, and what is a fair price for them. I don't see why I should teach him what is in fashion and what is not. A doctor does not ask you what kind of operation you want and what price you will pay for it. But I really believe these outfitter people would let me run about London wearing white cotton gloves and a plaid comforter without lifting a finger to prevent me.

And, by the bye, that reminds me of a scandalous trick these salesmen will play you. Sometimes they have not the thing you want, and then they make you buy other things. I happen to have, through no fault of my own, a very small head, and consequently for one long summer I wore a little boy's straw hat about London with the colours of a Paddington Board School, simply because a rascal outfitter hadn't my size in a proper kind of headgear, and induced me to buy the thing by specious representations. He must have known perfectly well it was not what I ought to wear. It seems never to enter into a shopman's code of honour that he ought to do his best for his customer. Since that, however, I have noticed lots of people about who have struck me in a new light as triumphs of the salesman, masterpieces in the art of incongruity; age in the garb of youth, corpulence put off with the size called "slender men's"; unhappy, gentle, quiet men with ties like oriflammes, breasts like a kingfisher's, and cataclysmal trouser patterns. Even so, if the shopkeeper had his will, should we all be. Those poor withered maiden ladies, too, who fill us with a kind of horror, with their juvenile curls, their girlish crudity of colouring, their bonnets, giddy, tottering, hectic. It overcomes me with remorse to think that I myself have accused them of vanity and folly. It overcomes me with pain to hear the thoughtless laugh aloud after them, in the public ways. For they are simply short-sighted trustful people, the myopic victims of the salesman and saleswoman. The little children gibe at them, pelt even.... And somewhere in the world a draper goes unhung.

However, the gloves are bought. I select a pair haphazard, and he pretends to perceive they fit perfectly by putting them over the back of my hand. I make him assure me of the fit, and then buy the pair and proceed to take my old ones off and put the new on grimly. If they split or the fingers are too long— glovemakers have the most erratic conceptions of the human

H. G. Wells

finger—I have to buy another pair.

But the trouble only begins when you have bought your thing. "Nothing more, sir?" he says. "Nothing," I say. "Braces?" he says. "No, thank you," I say. "Collars, cuffs?" He looks at mine swiftly but keenly, and with an unendurable suspicion.

He goes on, item after item. Am I in rags, that I should endure this thing? And I get sick of my everlasting "No, thank you"— the monotony shows up so glaringly against his kaleidoscope variety. I feel all the unutterable pettiness, the mean want of enterprise of my poor little purchase compared with the catholic fling he suggests. I feel angry with myself for being thus played upon, furiously angry with him. "*No, no*!" I say.

"These tie-holders are new." He proceeds to show me his infernal tie-holders. "They prevent the tie puckering," he says with his eye on mine. It's no good. "How much?" I say.

This whets him to further outrage. "Look here, my man!" I say at last, goaded to it, "I came here for gloves. After endless difficulties I at last induced you to let me have gloves. I have also been intimidated, by the most shameful hints and insinuations, into buying that *beastly* tie-holder. I'm not a child that I don't know my own needs. Now *will* you let me go? How much do you want?"

That usually checks him.

The above is a fair specimen of a shopman—a favourable rendering. There are other things they do, but I simply cannot write about them because it irritates me so to think of them. One infuriating manoeuvre is to correct your pronunciation. Another is to make a terrible ado about your name and address—even when it is quite a well-known name.

After I have bought things at a shop I am quite unfit for social intercourse. I have to go home and fume. There was a time when Euphemia would come and discuss my purchase with a certain levity, but on one occasion....

Some day these shopmen will goad me too far. It's almost my only consolation, indeed, to think what I am going to do when I do break out. There is a salesman somewhere in the world, he going on his way and I on mine, who will, I know, prove my last straw. It may be he will read this—amused—recking little of the mysteries of fate.... Is killing a salesman murder, like killing a human being?

THE BOOK OF CURSES

Professor Gargoyle, you must understand, has travelled to and fro in the earth, culling flowers of speech: a kind of recording angel he is, but without any sentimental tears. To be plain, he studies swearing. His collection, however, only approaches completeness in the western departments of European language. Going eastward he found such an appalling and tropical luxuriance of these ornaments as to despair at last altogether of even a representative selection. "They do not curse," he says, "at door-handles, and shirt-studs, and such other trifles as will draw down the meagre discharge of an Occidental, but when they do begin—

"I hired a promising-looking man at Calcutta, and after a month or so refused to pay his wages. He was unable to get at me with the big knife he carried, because the door was locked, so he sat on his hams outside under the verandah, from a quarter-past six in the morning until nearly ten, cursing—cursing in one steady unbroken flow—an astonishing spate of blasphemy. First he cursed my family, from me along the female line back to Eve, and then, having toyed with me personally for a little while, he started off along the line of my possible posterity to my remotest great-grandchildren. Then he cursed me by this and that. My hand ached taking it down, he was so very rich. It was a perfect anthology of Bengali blasphemy—vivid, scorching, and variegated. Not two alike. And then he turned about and dealt with different parts of me. I was really very fortunate in him. Yet it was depressing to think that all this was from one man, and that there are six hundred million people in Asia."

"Naturally," said the Professor in answer to my question, "these investigations involve a certain element of danger. The first condition of curse-collecting is to be unpopular, especially in the East, where comminatory swearing alone is practised, and you have to offend a man very grievously to get him to disgorge his treasure. In this country, except among ladies in comparatively humble circumstances, anything like this fluent, explicit, detailed, and sincere cursing, aimed, missile-fashion, at a personal enemy, is not found. It was quite common a few centuries ago; indeed, in the Middle Ages it was part of the recognised procedure. Aggrieved parties would issue a father's curse, an orphan's curse, and so forth, much as we should take out a county court summons. And it played a large part in ecclesiastical policy too. At one time the entire Church militant here on earth was swearing in unison, and the Latin tongue, at the Republic of Venice—a very splendid and imposing spectacle. It seems to me a pity to let these old customs die out so completely. I estimate that more than half these Gothic forms have altogether passed out of memory. There must have been some splendid things in Erse and Gaelic too; for the Celtic mind, with its more vivid sense of colour, its quicker transitions, and deeper emotional quality, has ever over-cursed the stolid Teuton. But it is all getting forgotten.

"Indeed, your common Englishman now scarcely curses at all. A more colourless and conventional affair than what in England is called swearing one can scarcely imagine. It is just common talk, with some half-dozen orthodox bad words dropped in here and there in the most foolish and illogical manner. Fancy having orthodox unorthodox words! I remember one day getting into a third-class smoking carriage on the Metropolitan Railway about one o'clock, and finding it full of rough working men. Everything they said was seasoned with one incredibly stupid adjective, and no doubt they thought they were very desperate characters. At last I asked them not to say that word again. One forthwith asked me 'What the—'—I really cannot quote these puerilities—'what the idiotic *cliche* that mattered to me?' So I looked at him quietly over my glasses, and I began. It was a revelation to these poor fellows. They sat open-mouthed, gasping. Then those that were nearest me began to edge away, and at the very next station they all bundled out of the carriage before the train stopped, as though I had some infectious disease. And the thing was just a rough imperfect rendering of some mere commonplaces, passing the time of day as it were, with which the heathen of Aleppo used to favour the servants of the American missionary. Indeed," said Professor Gargoyle, "if it were not for women there would be nothing in England that one could speak of as swearing at all."

"I say," said I, "is not that rather rough on the ladies?"

"Not at all; they have agreed to consider certain words, for no very good reason, bad words. It is a pure convention; it has little or nothing to do with the actual meaning, because for every one of these bad words there is a paraphrase or synonym considered to be quite suitable for polite ears. Hence the feeblest creature can always produce a sensation by breaking the taboo. But women are learning how to undo this error of theirs now. The word 'damn,' for instance, is, I hear, being admitted freely into the boudoir and feminine conversation; it is even considered a rather prudish thing to object to this word. Now, men, especially feeble men, hate doing things that women do. As a consequence, men who go about saying 'damn' are now regarded by their fellow-men as only a shade less effeminate than those who go about saying 'nasty' and 'horrid.' The subtler sex will not be long in noticing what has happened to this objectionable word. When they do they will, of course, forthwith take up all the others. It will be a little startling perhaps at first, but in the end there will be no swearing left. I have no doubt there will be those who will air their petty wit on the pioneer women, but where a martyr is wanted a woman can always be found to offer herself. She will clothe herself in cursing, like the ungodly, and perish in that Nessus shirt, a martyr to pure language. And then this dull cad swearing—a mere unnecessary affectation of coarseness—will disappear. And a very good job too.

"There is a pretty department of the subject which I might call grace swearing. 'Od's fish,' cried the king, when he saw the man climbing Salisbury spire; 'he shall have a patent for it—no one else shall do it.' One might call such little things Wardour Street curses. 'Od's bodkins' is a ladylike form, and 'Od's possles' a variety I met in the British Museum. Every gentleman once upon a time aspired to have his own particular grace curse, just as he liked to have his crest, and his bookplate, and his characteristic signature. It fluttered pleasantly into his conversation, as Mr. Whistler's butterfly comes into his pictures—a signature and a delight. 'Od's butterfly!' I have sometimes thought of a little book of grace-words and heraldic curses, printed with wide margins on the best of paper. Its covers should be of soft red leather, stamped with little gold flowers. It might be made a birthday book, or a pocket diary—'Daily Invocations.'

"Coming back to wrathy swearing, I must confess I am sorry to see it decay. It was such a thoroughly hygienic and moral practice. You see, if anything annoying happens to a man, or if any powerful emotion seizes him, his brain under the irritation begins to disengage energy at a tremendous rate. He has to use all his available force of control in keeping the energy in. Some of it will leak away into the nerves of his face and distort his features, some may set his tear-glands at work, some may travel down his vagus nerve and inhibit his heart's action so that he faints, or upset the blood-vessels in his head and give him a stroke. Or if he pens it up, without its reaching any of these vents, it may rise at last to flood-level, and you will have violent assaults, the breaking of furniture, 'murther' even. For all this energy a good flamboyant, ranting swear is Nature's outlet. All primitive men and most animals swear. It is an emotional shunt. Your cat swears at you because she does not want to scratch your face. And the horse, because he cannot swear, drops dead. So you see my reason for regretting the decay of this excellent and most wholesome practice....

H. G. Wells

"However, I must be getting on. Just now I am travelling about London paying cabmen their legal fares. Sometimes one picks up a new variant, though much of it is merely stereo."

And with that, flinging a playful curse at me, he disappeared at once into the tobacco smoke from which I had engendered him. An amusing and cheerful person on the whole, though I will admit his theme was a little undesirable.

DUNSTONE'S DEAR LADY

The story of Dunstone is so slight, so trivial in its cardinal incidents, such a business of cheap feathers and bits of ribbon on the surface, that I should hesitate to tell it, were it not for its Inwardness, what one might call the symbolism of the thing. Frankly, I do not clearly see what that symbolism is, but I feel it hovering in some indefinable way whenever I recall his case. It is one of those things that make a man extend his arm and twiddle his fingers, and say, blinking, "Like *that*, you know." So do not imagine for one moment that this is a shallow story, simply because it is painted, so to speak, not in heart's blood but in table claret.

Dunstone was a strong, quiet kind of man—a man of conspicuous mediocrity, and rising rapidly, therefore, in his profession. He was immensely industrious, and a little given to melancholia in private life. He smoked rather too many cigars, and took his social occasions seriously. He dressed faultlessly, with a scrupulous elimination of style. Unlike Mr. Grant Allen's ideal man, he was not constitutionally a lover; indeed, he seemed not to like the ordinary girl at all—found her either too clever or too shallow, lacking a something. I don't think *he* knew quite what it was. Neither do I—it is a case for extended hand and twiddling fingers. Moreover, I don't think the ordinary girl took to Dunstone very much.

He suffered, I fancy, from a kind of mental greyness; he was all subtle tones; the laughter of girls jarred upon him; foolish smartness or amiable foolishness got on his nerves; he detested,

H. G. Wells

with equal sincerity, bright dressing, artistic dabbling, piety, and the glow of health. And when, as his confidential friend—confidential, that is, so far as his limits allowed—I heard that he intended to marry, I was really very much surprised.

I expected something quintessential; I was surprised to find she was a visiting governess. Harringay, the artist, thought there was nothing in her, but Sackbut, the art critic, was inclined to admire her bones. For my own part, I took rather a liking to her. She was small and thin, and, to be frank, I think it was because she hardly got enough to eat—of the delicate food she needed. She was shabby, too, dressed in rusty mourning—she had recently lost her mother. But she had a sweet, low voice, a shrinking manner, rather a graceful carriage, I thought, and, though she spoke rarely, all she said was sweet and sane. She struck me as a refined woman in a blatant age. The general effect of her upon me was favourable; upon Dunstone it was tremendous. He lost a considerable proportion of his melancholia, and raved at times like a common man. He called her in particular his "Dear Lady" and his "Sweet Lady," things that I find eloquent of what he found in her. What that was I fancy I understand, and yet I cannot say it quite. One has to resort to the extended arm and fingers vibratile.

Before he married her—which he did while she was still in half-mourning—there was anxiety about her health, and I understood she needed air and exercise and strengthening food. But she recovered rapidly after her marriage, her eyes grew brighter, we saw less of Sackbut's "delicious skeleton." And then, in the strangest way, she began to change. It is none of my imagining; I have heard the change remarked upon by half a dozen independent observers. Yet you would think a girl of three-and-twenty (as she certainly was) had attained her development as a woman. I have heard her compared to a winter bud, cased in its sombre scales, until the sun shone, and the warm, moist winds began to blow. I noticed first that the delicate outline of her cheek was filling, and then came the time when she reverted to colour in her dress.

Her first essays were charitably received. Her years of struggle, her year of mourning, had no doubt dwarfed her powers in this direction; presently her natural good taste would reassert itself. But the next effort and the next were harder to explain. It was not the note of nervousness or inexperience we saw; there was an undeniable decision, and not a token of shame. The little black winter bud grew warm-coloured above, and burst suddenly into extravagant outlines and chromatic confusion. Harringay, who is a cad, first put what we were all feeling into words. "I've just seen Dunstone and his donah," he said. Clearly she was one of those rare women who cannot dress. And that was not all. A certain buoyancy, hitherto unsuspected, crept into her manner, as the corpuscles multiplied in her veins—an archness. She talked more, and threw up a spray of playfulness. And, with a growing energy, she began to revise the exquisite aesthetic balance of Dunstone's house. She even enamelled a chair.

For a year or so I was in the East. When I returned Mrs. Dunstone amazed me. In some odd way she had grown, she had positively grown. She was taller, broader, brighter—infinitely brighter. She wore a diamond brooch in the afternoon. The "delicious skeleton" had vanished in plumpness. She moved with emphasis. Her eye—which glittered—met mine bravely, and she talked as one who would be heard. In the old days you saw nothing but a rare timid glance from under the pretty lids. She talked now of this and that, of people of "good family," and the difficulty of getting a suitable governess for her little boy. She said she objected to meeting people "one would not care to invite to one's house." She swamped me with tea and ruled the conversation, so that Dunstone and I, who were once old friends, talked civil twaddle for the space of one hour—theatres, concerts, and assemblies chiefly—and then parted again. The furniture had all been altered—there were two "cosy nooks" in the room after the recipe in the *Born Lady*. It was plain to me, it is plain to everyone, I find, that Mrs. Dunstone is, in the sun of prosperity, rapidly developing an extremely florid vulgarity. And afterwards I discovered that she had forgotten her music, and evidently enjoyed her meals. Yet I for one can witness that five years ago there was *that* about her—I can only extend my arm with quivering digits. But it was something very sweet and dainty, something that made her white and thoughtful, and marked her off from the rest of womankind. I sometimes fancy it may have been anaemia in part, but it was certainly poverty and mourning in the main.

You may think that this is a story of disillusionment. When I first heard the story, I thought so too. But, so far as Dunstone goes, that is not the case. It is rare that I see him now, but the other day we smoked two cigars apiece together. And in a moment of confidence he spoke of her. He said how anxious he felt for her health, called her his "Dainty Little Lady," and spoke of the coarseness of other women. I am afraid this is not a very eventful story, and yet there is *that*—That very convenient gesture, an arm protruded and flickering fingers, conveys my meaning best. Perhaps you will understand.

EUPHEMIA'S NEW ENTERTAINMENT

Euphemia has great ideas of putting people at their ease, a thousand little devices for thawing the very stiffest among them with a home-like glow. Far be it from me to sing her praises, but I must admit that at times she is extremely successful in this—at times almost too successful. That tea-cake business, for instance. No doubt it's a genial expedient to make your guests toast his own tea-cake: down he must go upon his knees upon your hearthrug, and his poses will melt away like the dews of the morning before the rising sun. Nevertheless, when it comes to roasting a gallant veteran like Major Augustus, deliberately roasting him, in spite of the facts that he has served his country nobly through thirty irksome years of peace, and that he admires Euphemia with a delicate fervour—roasting him, I say, alive, as if he were a Strasburg goose, or suddenly affixing a delicate young genius to the hither end of a toasting-fork while he is in the midst of a really very subtle and tender conversation, the limits of social warmth seem to be approaching dangerously near. However, this scarcely concerns Euphemia's new entertainment.

This new entertainment is modelling in clay. Euphemia tells me it is to be quite the common thing this winter. It is intended especially for the evening, after a little dinner. As the reader is aware, the evening after a little dinner is apt to pall. A certain placid contentment creeps over people. I don't know in what organ originality resides; but it's a curious thing, and one I must leave to the consideration of psychologists, that people's output of original remarks appears to be obstructed in some

H. G. Wells

way after these gastronomic exercises. Then a little dinner always confirms my theory of the absurdity of polygonal conversation. Music and songs, too, have their drawbacks, especially gay songs; they invariably evoke a vaporous melancholy. Card-playing Euphemia objects to because her uncle, the dean, is prominent in connection with some ridiculous association for the suppression of gambling; and in what are called "games" no rational creature esteeming himself an immortal soul would participate. In this difficulty it was that Euphemia—decided, I fancy, by the possession of certain really very becoming aprons—took up this business of clay-modelling.

You have a lump of greyish clay and a saucer of water and certain small tools of wood (for which I cannot discover the slightest use in the world) given you, and Euphemia puts on a very winning bib. Then, moistening the clay until it acquires sufficient plasticity, and incidentally splashing your cuffs and coat-sleeves with an agreeably light tinted mud, you set to work. At first people are a little disgusted at the apparent dirtiness of the employment, and also perhaps rather diffident. The eldest lady says weakly deprecatory things, and the feeblest male is jocular after his wont. But it is remarkable how soon the charm of this delightful occupation seizes hold of you. For really the sensations of moulding this plastic matter into shape are wonderfully and quite unaccountably pleasing. It is ever so much easier than drawing things—"anyone can do it," as the advertisement people say—and the work is so much more substantial in its effects. Technical questions arise. In moulding a head, do you take a lump and fine it down, or do you dab on the features after the main knob of it is shaped?

So soon as your guests realise the plastic possibilities before them, a great silence, a delicious absorption comes over them. Some rash person states that he is moulding an Apollo, or a vase, or a bust of Mr. Gladstone, or an elephant, or some such animal. The wiser ones go to work in a speculative spirit, aiming secretly at this perhaps, but quite willing to go on with that, if Providence so wills it. Buddhas are good subjects; there is a certain genial rotundity not difficult to attain, and the pyramidal build of the idol is well suited to the material. You can start a Buddha, and hedge to make it a loaf of bread if the features are unsatisfactory. For slender objects a skeletal substructure of bent hairpins or matches is advisable. The innate egotism of the human animal becomes very conspicuous. "His tail is too large," says the lady with the fish, in self-criticism. "I haven't put his tail on yet—that's his trunk," answers the young man with the elephant.

It's a pretty sight to see the first awakening of the artistic passion in your guests—the flush of discovery, the glow of innocent pride as the familiar features of Mr. Gladstone emerge from the bust of Clytie. An accidental stroke of the thumbnail develops new marvels of expression. (By the bye, it's just as well to forbid deliberate attempts at portraiture.) And I know no more becoming expression for everyone than the look of intent and pleasing effort—a divine touch almost—that comes over the common man modelling. For my own part, I feel a being infinitely my own superior when I get my fingers upon the clay. And, incidentally, how much pleasanter this is than writing articles—to see the work grow altogether under your hands; to begin with the large masses and finish with the details, as every artist should! Just to show how easy the whole thing is, I append a little sketch of the first work I ever did. I had had positively no previous instruction. Unfortunately the left ear of the animal—a cat, by the bye—has fallen off. (The figure to the left is the back view of a Buddha.)

However, I have said enough to show the charm of the new amusement. It will prove a boon to many a troubled hostess. The material is called modelling-clay, and one may buy it of any dealer in artists' materials, several pounds for sixpence. This has to be renewed at intervals, as a good deal is taken away by the more careless among your guests upon their clothes.

H. G. Wells

FOR FREEDOM OF SPELLING

THE DISCOVERY OF AN ART

It is curious that people do not grumble more at having to spell correctly. Yet one may ask, Do we not a little over-estimate the value of orthography? This is a natural reflection enough when the maker of artless happy phrases has been ransacking the dictionary for some elusive wretch of a word which in the end proves to be not yet naturalised, or technical, or a mere local vulgarity; yet one does not often hear the idea canvassed in polite conversation. Dealers in small talk, of the less prolific kind, are continually falling back upon the silk hat or dress suit, or some rule of etiquette or other convention as a theme, but spelling seems to escape them. The suspicion seems quaint, but one may almost fancy that an allusion to spelling savoured a little of indelicacy. It must be admitted, though where the scruples come from would be hard to say, that there is a certain diffidence even here in broaching my doubts in the matter. For some inexplicable reason spelling has become mixed up with moral feeling. One cannot pretend to explain things in a little paper of this kind; the fact is so. Spelling is not appropriate or inappropriate, elegant or inelegant; it is right or wrong. We do not greatly blame a man for turn-down collars when the vogue is erect; nor, in these liberal days, for theological eccentricity; but we esteem him "Nithing" and an outcast if he but drop a "p" from opportunity. It is not an anecdote, but a scandal, if we say a man cannot spell his own name. There is only one thing esteemed worse before we come to the deadly crimes, and that is the softening of language by dropping the aspirate.

After all, it is an unorthodox age. We are all horribly afraid of being bourgeois, and unconventionality is the ideal of every respectable person. It is strange that we should cling so steadfastly to correct spelling. Yet again, one can partly understand the business, if one thinks of the little ways of your schoolmaster and schoolmistress. This sanctity of spelling is stamped upon us in our earliest years. The writer recalls a period of youth wherein six hours a week were given to the study of spelling, and four hours to all other religious instruction. So important is it, that a writer who cannot spell is almost driven to abandon his calling, however urgent the thing he may have to say, or his need of the incidentals of fame. Yet in the crisis of such a struggle rebellious thoughts may arise. Even this: Why, after all, should correct spelling be the one absolutely essential literary merit? For it is less fatal for an ambitious scribe to be as dull as Hoxton than to spell in diverse ways.

Yet correct spelling of English has not been traced to revelation; there was no grammatical Sinai, with a dictionary instead of tables of stone. Indeed, we do not even know certainly when correct spelling began, which word in the language was first spelt the right way, and by whom. Correct spelling may have been evolved, or it may be the creation of some master mind. Its inventor, if it had an inventor, is absolutely forgotten. Thomas Cobbett would have invented it, but that he was born more than two centuries too late, poor man. All that we certainly know is that, contemporaneously with the rise of extreme Puritanism, the belief in orthography first spread among Elizabethan printers, and with the Hanoverian succession the new doctrine possessed the whole length and breadth of the land. At that time the world passed through what extension lecturers call, for no particular reason, the classical epoch. Nature—as, indeed, all the literature manuals testify—was in the remotest background then of human thought. The human mind, in a mood of the severest logic, brought everything to the touchstone of an orderly reason; the conception of "correctness" dominated all mortal affairs. For instance, one's natural hair with its vagaries of rat's tails, duck's tails, errant curls, and baldness, gave place to an orderly wig, or was at least decently powdered. The hoop remedied the deficiencies of the feminine form, and the gardener clipped his yews into respectability. All poetry was written to one measure in those days, and a Royal Academy with a lady member was inaugurated that art might become at least decent. Dictionaries began. The crowning glory of Hanoverian literature was a Great Lexicographer.

In those days it was believed that the spelling of every English word had been settled for all time. Thence to the present day, though the severities then inaugurated, so far as metre and artistic composition are concerned, been generously relaxed— though we have had a Whistler, a Walt Whitman, and a Wagner—the rigours of spelling have continued unabated. There is just one right way of spelling, and all others are held to be not simply inelegant or undesirable, but wrong; and unorthodox spelling, like original morality, goes hand in hand with shame.

Yet even at the risk of shocking the religious convictions of some, may not one ask whether spelling is in truth a matter of right and wrong at all? Might it not rather be an art? It is too much to advocate the indiscriminate sacking of the alphabet, but yet it seems plausible that there is a happy medium between a reckless debauch of errant letters and our present dead rigidity. For some words at anyrate may there not be sometimes one way of spelling a little happier, sometimes another? We do something of this sort even now with our "phantasy" and "fantasie," and we might do more. How one would spell this word or that would become, if this latitude were conceded, a subtle anxiety of the literary exquisite. People are scarcely prepared to realise what shades of meaning may be got by such a simple device. Let us take a simple instance. You write, let us say, to all your cousins, many of your friends, and even, it may be, to this indifferent intimate and that familiar enemy, "My dear So-and-so." But at times you feel even as you write, sometimes, that there is something too much and sometimes something lacking. You may even get so far in the right way occasionally as to write, "My dr. So-and-so," when your heart is chill. And people versed in the arts of social intercourse know the subtle insult of misspelling a person's name, or flicking it off flippantly with a mere waggling wipe of the pen. But these are mere beginnings.

Let the reader take a pen in hand and sit down and write, "My very dear wife." Clean, cold, and correct this is, speaking of orderly affection, settled and stereotyped long ago. In such letters is butcher's meat also "very dear." Try now, "Migh verrie deare Wyfe." Is it not immediately infinitely more soft and tender? Is there not something exquisitely pleasant in lingering over those redundant letters, leaving each word, as it were, with a reluctant caress? Such spelling is a soft, domestic, lovingly wasteful use of material. Or, again, if you have no wife, or object to an old-fashioned conjugal tenderness, try "Mye owne sweete dearrest Marrie." There is the tremble of a tenderness no mere arrangement of trim everyday letters can express in those double *r's*. "Sweete" my ladie must be; sweet! why pump-water and inferior champagne, spirits of nitrous ether and pancreatic juice are "sweet." For my own part I always spell so, with lots of *f's* and *g's* and such like tailey, twirley, loopey things, when my heart is in the tender vein. And I hold that a man who will not do so, now he has been shown how to do it, is, in plain English, neither more nor less than a prig. The advantages of a varied spelling of names are very great. Industrious, rather than intelligent, people have given not a little time, and such minds as they have, to the discussion of the right spelling of our great poet's name. But he himself never dreamt of tying himself down to one presentation of himself, and was—we have his hand for it— Shakespeare, Shakspear, Shakespear, Shakspeare, and so forth, as the mood might be. It would be almost as reasonable to debate whether Shakespeare smiled or frowned. My dear friend Simmongues is the same. He is "Sims," a mere slash of the pen, to those he scorns, Simmonds or Simmongs to his familiars, and Simmons, A.T. Simmons, Esq., to all Europe.

H. G. Wells

From such mere introductory departures from precision, such petty escapades as these, we would we might seduce the reader into an utter debauch of spelling. But a sudden Maenad dance of the letters on the page, gleeful and iridescent spelling, a wild rush and procession of howling vowels and clattering consonants, might startle the half-won reader back into orthodoxy. Besides, there is another reader—the printer's reader—to consider. For if an author let his wit run to these matters, he must write elaborate marginal exhortations to this authority, begging his mercy, to let the little flowers of spelling alone. Else the plough of that Philistine's uniformity will utterly root them out.

Such high art of spelling as is thus hinted at is an art that has still to gather confidence and brave the light of publicity. A few, indeed, practise it secretly for love—in letters and on spare bits of paper. But, for the most part, people do not know that there is so much as an art of spelling possible; the tyranny of orthography lies so heavily on the land. Your common editors and their printers are a mere orthodox spelling police, and at the least they rigorously blot out all the delightful frolics of your artist in spelling before his writings reach the public eye. But commonly, as I have proved again and again, the slightest lapse into rococo spelling is sufficient to secure the rejection of a manuscript without further ado.

And to end,—a word about Phonographers. It may be that my title has led the reader to anticipate some mention of these before. They are a kind of religious sect, a heresy from the orthodox spelling. They bind one another by their mysteries and a five-shilling subscription in a "soseiti to introduis an impruvd method of spelinj." They come across the artistic vision, they and their Soseiti, with an altogether indefinable offence. Perhaps the essence of it is the indescribable meanness of their motive. For this phonography really amounts to a study of the cheapest way of spelling words. These phonographers are sweaters of the Queen's English, living meanly on the selvage of honest mental commerce by clipping the coin of thought. But enough of them. They are mentioned here only to be disavowed. They would substitute one narrow orthodoxy for another, and I would unfold the banner of freedom. Spell, my brethren, as you will! Awake, arise, O language living in chains; let Butter's spelling be our Bastille! So with a prophetic vision of liberated words pouring out of the dungeons of a spelling-book, this plea for freedom concludes. What trivial arguments there are for a uniform spelling I must leave the reader to discover. This is no place to carp against the liberation I foresee, with the glow of the dawn in my eyes.

H. G. Wells

INCIDENTAL THOUGHTS ON A BALD HEAD

I was asked to go, quite suddenly, and found myself there before I had time to think of what it might be. I understood her to say it was a meeting of some "Sunday society," some society that tried to turn the Sabbath from a day of woe to a day of rejoicing. "St. George's Hall, Langham Place," a cab, and there we were. I thought they would be picturesque Pagans. But the entertainment was the oddest it has ever been my lot to see, a kind of mystery. The place was dark, except for a big circle of light on a screen, and a dismal man with a long stick was talking about the effects of alcohol on your muscles. He talked and talked, and people went to sleep all about us. Euphemia's face looked so very pretty in the dim light that I tried to talk to her and hold her hand, but she only said "Ssh!" And then they began showing pictures on the screen—the most shocking things!—stomachs, and all that kind of thing. They went on like that for an hour, and then there was a lot of thumping with umbrellas, and they turned the lights up and we went home. Curious way of spending Sunday afternoon, is it not?

But you may imagine I had a dismal time all that hour. I understood the people about me were Sceptics, the kind of people who don't believe things—a singular class, and, I am told, a growing one. These excellent people, it seems, have conscientious objections to going to chapel or church, but at the same time the devotional habit of countless generations of pious forerunners is strong in them. Consequently they have invented things like these lectures to go to, with a professor instead of a priest, and a lantern slide of a stomach by way of altar-piece; and alcohol they make their Devil, and their god is Hygiene—a curious and instructive case of mental inertia. I understand, too, there are several other temples of this Cult in London—South Place Chapel and Essex Hall, for instance, where they worship the Spirit of the Innermost. But the thing that struck me so oddly was the number of bald heads glimmering faintly in the reflected light from the lantern circle. And that set me thinking upon a difficulty I have never been able to surmount.

You see these people, and lots of other people, too, believe in a thing they call Natural Selection. They think, as part of that belief, that men are descended from hairy simian ancestors; assert that even a hundred thousand years ago the ancestor was hairy—hairy, heavy, and almost as much a brute as if he lived in Mr. Arthur Morrison's Whitechapel. For my own part I think it a pretty theory, and would certainly accept it were it not for one objection. The thing I cannot understand is how our ancestor lost that hair. I see no reason why he should not have kept his hair on. According to the theory of natural selection, materially favourable variations survive, unfavourable disappear; the only way in which the loss is to be accounted for is by explaining it as advantageous; but where is the advantage of losing your hair? The disadvantages appear to me to be innumerable. A thick covering of hair, like that of a Capuchin monkey, would be an invaluable protection against sudden changes of temperature, far better than any clothing can be. Had I that, for instance, I should be rid of the perpetual cold in the head that so disfigures my life; and the multitudes who die annually of chills, bronchitis, and consumption, and most of those who suffer from rheumatic pains, neuralgia, and so forth, would not so die and suffer. And in the past, when clothing was less perfect and firing a casual commodity, the disadvantages of losing hair were all the greater. In very hot countries hair is perhaps even more important in saving the possessor from the excessive glare of the sun. Before the invention of the hat, thick hair on the head at least was absolutely essential to save the owner of the skull from sunstroke. That, perhaps, explains why the hair has been retained there, and why it is going now that we have hats, but it certainly does not explain why it has gone from the rest of the body.

One—remarkably weak—explanation has been propounded: an appeal to our belief in human vanity. He picked it out by the roots, because he thought he was prettier without. But that is no reason at all. Suppose he did, it would not affect his children. Professor Weismann has at least convinced scientific people of this: that the characters acquired by a parent are rarely, if ever, transmitted to its offspring. An individual given to such wanton denudation would simply be at a disadvantage with his decently covered fellows, would fall behind in the race of life, and perish with his kind. Besides, if man has been at such pains to uncover his skin, why have quite a large number of the most respected among us such a passionate desire to have it covered up again?

Yet that is the only attempted explanation I have ever come upon, and the thing has often worried me. I think it is just as probably a change in dietary. I have noticed that most of your vegetarians are shock-headed, ample-bearded men, and I have heard the Ancestor was vegetarian. Or it may be, I sometimes fancy, a kind of inherent disposition on the part of your human animal to dwindle. That came back in my memory vividly as I looked at the long rows of Sceptics, typical Advanced people, and marked their glistening crania. I recalled other losses. Here is Humanity, thought I, growing hairless, growing bald, growing toothless, unemotional, irreligious, losing the end joint of the little toe, dwindling in its osseous structures, its jawbone and brow ridges, losing all the full, rich curvatures of its primordial beauty.

It seems almost like what the scientific people call a Law. And by strenuous efforts the creature just keeps pace with his losses—devises clothes, wigs, artificial teeth, paddings, shoes— what civilised being could use his bare feet for his ordinary locomotion? Imagine him on a furze-sprinkled golf links. Then stays, an efficient substitute for the effete feminine backbone. So the thing goes on. Long ago his superficies became artificial, and now the human being shrinks like a burning cigar, and the figure he has abandoned remains distended with artificial ashes, dead dry protections against the exposures he so unaccountably fears. Will he go on shrinking, I wonder?— become at last a mere lurking atomy in his own recesses, a kind of hermit crab, the bulk of him a complex mechanism, a thing of rags and tatters and papier-mache, stolen from the earth and the plant-world and his fellow beasts? And at last may he not disappear altogether, none missing him, and a democracy of honest machinery, neatly clad and loaded up with sound principles of action, walk to and fro in a regenerate world? Thus it was my mind went dreaming in St. George's Hall. But presently, as I say, came the last word about stomachs, and the bald men woke up, rattled their umbrellas, said it was vastly interesting, and went toddling off home in an ecstasy of advanced Liberalism. And we two returned to the place whence we came.

H. G. Wells

OF A BOOK UNWRITTEN

Accomplished literature is all very well in its way, no doubt, but much more fascinating to the contemplative man are the books that have not been written. These latter are no trouble to hold; there are no pages to turn over. One can read them in bed on sleepless nights without a candle. Turning to another topic, primitive man in the works of the descriptive anthropologist is certainly a very entertaining and quaint person, but the man of the future, if we only had the facts, would appeal to us more strongly. Yet where are the books? As Ruskin has said somewhere, *a propos* of Darwin, it is not what man has been, but what he will be, that should interest us.

The contemplative man in his easy-chair, pondering this saying, suddenly beholds in the fire, through the blue haze of his pipe, one of these great unwritten volumes. It is large in size, heavy in lettering, seemingly by one Professor Holzkopf, presumably Professor at Weissnichtwo. "The Necessary Characters of the Man of the Remote Future deduced from the Existing Stream of Tendency" is the title. The worthy Professor is severely scientific in his method, and deliberate and cautious in his deductions, the contemplative man discovers as he pursues his theme, and yet the conclusions are, to say the least, remarkable. We must figure the excellent Professor expanding the matter at great length, voluminously technical, but the contemplative man—since he has access to the only copy—is clearly at liberty to make such extracts and abstracts as he chooses for the unscientific reader. Here, for instance, is something of practicable lucidity that he considers admits of quotation. "The theory of evolution," writes the Professor, "is now universally accepted by zoologists and botanists, and it is applied unreservedly to man. Some question, indeed, whether it fits his soul, but all agree it accounts for his body. Man, we are assured, is descended from ape-like ancestors, moulded by circumstances into men, and these apes again were derived from ancestral forms of a lower order, and so up from the primordial protoplasmic jelly. Clearly then, man, unless the order of the universe has come to an end, will undergo further modification in the future, and at last cease to be man, giving rise to some other type of animated being. At once the fascinating question arises, What will this being be? Let us consider for a little the plastic influences at work upon our species.

"Just as the bird is the creature of the wing, and is all moulded and modified to flying, and just as the fish is the creature that swims, and has had to meet the inflexible conditions of a problem in hydrodynamics, so man is the creature of the brain; he will live by intelligence, and not by physical strength, if he live at all. So that much that is purely 'animal' about him is being, and must be, beyond all question, suppressed in his ultimate development. Evolution is no mechanical tendency making for perfection, according to the ideas current in the year of grace 1897; it is simply the continual adaptation of plastic life, for good or evil, to the circumstances that surround it.... We notice this decay of the animal part around us now, in the loss of teeth and hair, in the dwindling hands and feet of men, in their smaller jaws, and slighter mouths and ears. Man now does by wit and machinery and verbal agreement what he once did by bodily toil; for once he had to catch his dinner, capture his wife, run away from his enemies, and continually exercise himself, for love of himself, to perform these duties well. But now all this is changed. Cabs, trains, trams, render speed unnecessary, the pursuit of food becomes easier; his wife is no longer hunted, but rather, in view of the crowded matrimonial market, seeks him out. One needs wits now to live, and physical activity is a drug, a snare even; it seeks artificial outlets, and overflows in games. Athleticism takes up

H. G. Wells

time and cripples a man in his competitive examinations, and in business. So is your fleshly man handicapped against his subtler brother. He is unsuccessful in life, does not marry. The better adapted survive."

The coming man, then, will clearly have a larger brain, and a slighter body than the present. But the Professor makes one exception to this. "The human hand, since it is the teacher and interpreter of the brain, will become constantly more powerful and subtle as the rest of the musculature dwindles."

Then in the physiology of these children of men, with their expanding brains, their great sensitive hands and diminishing bodies, great changes were necessarily worked. "We see now," says the Professor, "in the more intellectual sections of humanity an increasing sensitiveness to stimulants, a growing inability to grapple with such a matter as alcohol, for instance. No longer can men drink a bottleful of port; some cannot drink tea; it is too exciting for their highly-wrought nervous systems. The process will go on, and the Sir Wilfrid Lawson of some near generation may find it his duty and pleasure to make the silvery spray of his wisdom tintinnabulate against the tea-tray. These facts lead naturally to the comprehension of others. Fresh raw meat was once a dish for a king. Now refined persons scarcely touch meat unless it is cunningly disguised. Again, consider the case of turnips; the raw root is now a thing almost uneatable, but once upon a time a turnip must have been a rare and fortunate find, to be torn up with delirious eagerness and devoured in ecstasy. The time will come when the change will affect all the other fruits of the earth. Even now, only the young of mankind eat apples raw—the young always preserving ancestral characteristics after their disappearance in the adult. Some day even boys will regard apples without emotion. The boy of the future, one must believe, will gaze on an apple with the same unspeculative languor with which he now regards a flint"—in the absence of a cat.

"Furthermore, fresh chemical discoveries came into action as modifying influences upon men. In the prehistoric period even, man's mouth had ceased to be an instrument for grasping food; it is still growing continually less prehensile, his front teeth are smaller, his lips thinner and less muscular; he has a new organ, a mandible not of irreparable tissue, but of bone and steel—a knife and fork. There is no reason why things should stop at partial artificial division thus afforded; there is every reason, on the contrary, to believe my statement that some cunning exterior mechanism will presently masticate and insalivate his dinner, relieve his diminishing salivary glands and teeth, and at last altogether abolish them."

Then what is not needed disappears. What use is there for external ears, nose, and brow ridges now? The two latter once protected the eye from injury in conflict and in falls, but in these days we keep on our legs, and at peace. Directing his thoughts in this way, the reader may presently conjure up a dim, strange vision of the latter-day face: "Eyes large, lustrous, beautiful, soulful; above them, no longer separated by rugged brow ridges, is the top of the head, a glistening, hairless dome, terete and beautiful; no craggy nose rises to disturb by its unmeaning shadows the symmetry of that calm face, no vestigial ears project; the mouth is a small, perfectly round aperture, toothless and gumless, jawless, unanimal, no futile emotions disturbing its roundness as it lies, like the harvest moon or the evening star, in the wide firmament of face." Such is the face the Professor beholds in the future.

Of course parallel modifications will also affect the body and limbs. "Every day so many hours and so much energy are required for digestion; a gross torpidity, a carnal lethargy, seizes on mortal men after dinner. This may and can be avoided. Man's knowledge of organic chemistry widens daily. Already he can supplement the gastric glands by artificial devices. Every doctor who administers physic implies that the bodily functions may be artificially superseded. We have pepsine, pancreatine, artificial gastric acid—I know not what like mixtures. Why, then, should not the stomach be ultimately superannuated altogether? A man who could not only leave his dinner to be cooked, but also leave it to be masticated and digested, would have vast social advantages over his food-digesting fellow. This is, let me remind you here, the calmest, most passionless, and scientific working out of the future forms of things from the data of the present. At this stage the following facts may perhaps stimulate your imagination. There can be no doubt that many of the Arthropods, a division of animals more ancient and even now more prevalent than the Vertebrata, have undergone more phylogenetic modification"—a beautiful phrase—"than even the most modified of vertebrated animals. Simple forms like the lobsters display a primitive structure parallel with that of the fishes. However, in such a form as the degraded 'Chondracanthus,' the structure has diverged far more widely from its original type than in man. Among some of these most highly modified crustaceans the whole of the alimentary canal—that is, all the food-digesting and food-absorbing parts—form a useless solid cord: the animal is nourished—it is a parasite—by absorption of the nutritive fluid in which it swims. Is there any absolute impossibility in supposing man to be destined for a similar change; to imagine him no longer dining, with unwieldy paraphernalia of servants and plates, upon food queerly dyed and distorted, but nourishing himself in elegant simplicity by immersion in a tub of nutritive fluid?

"There grows upon the impatient imagination a building, a dome of crystal, across the translucent surface of which flushes of the most glorious and pure prismatic colours pass and fade and change. In the centre of this transparent chameleon-tinted dome is a circular white marble basin filled with some clear, mobile, amber liquid, and in this plunge and float strange beings. Are they birds?

"They are the descendants of man—at dinner. Watch them as they hop on their hands—a method of progression advocated already by Bjornsen—about the pure white marble floor. Great hands they have, enormous brains, soft, liquid, soulful eyes. Their whole muscular system, their legs, their abdomens, are shrivelled to nothing, a dangling, degraded pendant to their minds."

The further visions of the Professor are less alluring.

"The animals and plants die away before men, except such as he preserves for his food or delight, or such as maintain a precarious footing about him as commensals and parasites. These vermin and pests must succumb sooner or later to his untiring inventiveness and incessantly growing discipline. When he learns (the chemists are doubtless getting towards the secret now) to do the work of chlorophyll without the plant, then his necessity for other animals and plants upon the earth will disappear. Sooner or later, where there is no power of resistance and no necessity, there comes extinction. In the last days man will be alone on the earth, and his food will be won by the chemist from the dead rocks and the sunlight.

"And—one may learn the full reason in that explicit and painfully right book, the *Data of Ethics*—the irrational fellowship of man will give place to an intellectual co-operation, and emotion fall within the scheme of reason. Undoubtedly it is a long time yet, but a long time is nothing in the face of eternity, and every man who dares think of these things must look eternity in the face."

Then the earth is ever radiating away heat into space, the Professor reminds us. And so at last comes a vision of earthly cherubim, hopping heads, great unemotional intelligences, and little hearts, fighting together perforce and fiercely against the cold that grips them tighter and tighter. For the world is cooling—slowly and inevitably it grows colder as the years roll by. "We must imagine these creatures," says the Professor, "in galleries and laboratories deep down in the bowels of the earth. The whole world will be snow-covered and piled with ice; all animals, all vegetation vanished, except this last branch of the tree of life. The last men have gone even deeper, following the diminishing heat of the planet, and vast metallic shafts and ventilators make way for the air they need."

So with a glimpse of these human tadpoles, in their deep close gallery, with their boring machinery ringing away, and artificial lights glaring and casting black shadows, the Professor's horoscope concludes. Humanity in dismal retreat before the cold, changed beyond recognition. Yet the Professor is reasonable enough, his facts are current science, his methods orderly. The contemplative man shivers at the prospect, starts up to poke the fire, and the whole of this remarkable book that is not written vanishes straightway in the smoke of his pipe. This is the great advantage of this unwritten literature: there is no bother in changing the books. The contemplative man consoles himself for the destiny of the species with the lost portion of Kubla Khan.

THE EXTINCTION OF MAN

It is part of the excessive egotism of the human animal that the bare idea of its extinction seems incredible to it. "A world without *us*!" it says, as a heady young Cephalaspis might have said it in the old Silurian sea. But since the Cephalaspis and the Coccosteus many a fine animal has increased and multiplied upon the earth, lorded it over land or sea without a rival, and passed at last into the night. Surely it is not so unreasonable to ask why man should be an exception to the rule. From the scientific standpoint at least any reason for such exception is hard to find.

No doubt man is undisputed master at the present time—at least of most of the land surface; but so it has been before with other animals. Let us consider what light geology has to throw upon this. The great land and sea reptiles of the Mesozoic period, for instance, seem to have been as secure as humanity is now in their pre-eminence. But they passed away and left no descendants when the new orders of the mammals emerged from their obscurity. So, too, the huge Titanotheria of the American continent, and all the powerful mammals of Pleistocene South America, the sabre-toothed lion, for instance, and the Machrauchenia suddenly came to a finish when they were still almost at the zenith of their rule. *And in no case does the record of the fossils show a really dominant species succeeded by its own descendants.* What has usually happened in the past appears to be the emergence of some type of animal hitherto rare and unimportant, and the extinction, not simply of the previously ruling species, but of most of the forms that

H. G. Wells

are at all closely related to it. Sometimes, indeed, as in the case of the extinct giants of South America, they vanished without any considerable rivals, victims of pestilence, famine, or, it may be, of that cumulative inefficiency that comes of a too undisputed life. So that the analogy of geology, at anyrate, is against this too acceptable view of man's certain tenure of the earth for the next few million years or so.

And, after all, even now man is by no means such a master of the kingdoms of life as he is apt to imagine. The sea, that mysterious nursery of living things, is for all practical purposes beyond his control. The low-water mark is his limit. Beyond that he may do a little with seine and dredge, murder a few million herrings a year as they come in to spawn, butcher his fellow air-breather, the whale, or haul now and then an unlucky king-crab or strange sea-urchin out of the deep water, in the name of science; but the life of the sea as a whole knows him not, plays out its slow drama of change and development unheeding him, and may in the end, in mere idle sport, throw up some new terrestrial denizens, some new competitor for space to live in and food to live upon, that will sweep him and all his little contrivances out of existence, as certainly and inevitably as he has swept away auk, bison, and dodo during the last two hundred years.

For instance, there are the Crustacea. As a group the crabs and lobsters are confined below the high-water mark. But experiments in air-breathing are no doubt in progress in this group—we already have tropical land-crabs—and as far as we know there is no reason why in the future these creatures should not increase in size and terrestrial capacity. In the past we have the evidence of the fossil *Paradoxides* that creatures of this kind may at least attain a length of six feet, and, considering their intense pugnacity, a crab of such dimensions would be as formidable a creature as one could well imagine. And their amphibious capacity would give them an advantage against us such as at present is only to be found in the case of the alligator or crocodile. If we imagine a shark that could raid out upon the land, or a tiger that could take refuge in the sea, we should have a fair suggestion of what a terrible monster a large predatory crab might prove. And so far as zoological science goes we must, at least, admit that such a creature is an evolutionary possibility.

Then, again, the order of the Cephalopods, to which belong the cuttle-fish and the octopus (sacred to Victor Hugo), may be, for all we can say to the contrary, an order with a future. Their kindred, the Gastropods, have, in the case of the snail and slug, learnt the trick of air-breathing. And not improbably there are even now genera of this order that have escaped the naturalist, or even well-known genera whose possibilities in growth and dietary are still unknown. Suppose some day a specimen of a new species is caught off the coast of Kent. It excites remark at a Royal Society soiree, engenders a Science Note or so, "A Huge Octopus!" and in the next year or so three or four other specimens come to hand, and the thing becomes familiar. "Probably a new and larger variety of *Octopus* so-and-so, hitherto supposed to be tropical," says Professor Gargoyle, and thinks he has disposed of it. Then conceive some mysterious boating accidents and deaths while bathing. A large animal of this kind coming into a region of frequent wrecks might so easily acquire a preferential taste for human nutriment, just as the Colorado beetle acquired a new taste for the common potato and gave up its old food-plants some years ago. Then perhaps a school or pack or flock of *Octopus gigas* would be found busy picking the sailors off a stranded ship, and then in the course of a few score years it might begin to stroll up the beaches and batten on excursionists. Soon it would be a common feature of the watering-places—possibly at last commoner than excursionists. Suppose such a creature were to appear—and it is, we repeat, a possibility, if perhaps a remote one—how could it be fought against? Something might be done by torpedoes; but, so far as our past knowledge goes, man has no means of seriously diminishing the numbers of any animal of the most rudimentary intelligence that made its fastness in the sea.

Even on land it is possible to find creatures that with a little

H. G. Wells

modification might become excessively dangerous to the human ascendency. Most people have read of the migratory ants of Central Africa, against which no man can stand. On the march they simply clear out whole villages, drive men and animals before them in headlong rout, and kill and eat every living creature they can capture. One wonders why they have not already spread the area of their devastations. But at present no doubt they have their natural checks, of ant-eating birds, or what not. In the near future it may be that the European immigrant, as he sets the balance of life swinging in his vigorous manner, may kill off these ant-eating animals, or otherwise unwittingly remove the checks that now keep these terrible little pests within limits. And once they begin to spread in real earnest, it is hard to see how their advance could be stopped. A world devoured by ants seems incredible now, simply because it is not within our experience; but a naturalist would have a dull imagination who could not see in the numerous species of ants, and in their already high intelligence, far more possibility of strange developments than we have in the solitary human animal. And no doubt the idea of the small and feeble organism of man, triumphant and omnipresent, would have seemed equally incredible to an intelligent mammoth or a palaeolithic cave bear.

And, finally, there is always the prospect of a new disease. As yet science has scarcely touched more than the fringe of the probabilities associated with the minute fungi that constitute our zymotic diseases. But the bacilli have no more settled down into their final quiescence than have men; like ourselves, they are adapting themselves to new conditions and acquiring new powers. The plagues of the Middle Ages, for instance, seem to have been begotten of a strange bacillus engendered under conditions that sanitary science, in spite of its panacea of drainage, still admits are imperfectly understood, and for all we know even now we may be quite unwittingly evolving some new and more terrible plague—a plague that will not take ten or twenty or thirty per cent., as plagues have done in the past, but the entire hundred.

No; man's complacent assumption of the future is too confident. We think, because things have been easy for mankind as a whole for a generation or so, we are going on to perfect comfort and security in the future. We think that we shall always go to work at ten and leave off at four, and have dinner at seven for ever and ever. But these four suggestions, out of a host of others, must surely do a little against this complacency. Even now, for all we can tell, the coming terror may be crouching for its spring and the fall of humanity be at hand. In the case of every other predominant animal the world has ever seen, I repeat, the hour of its complete ascendency has been the eve of its entire overthrow. But if some poor story-writing man ventures to figure this sober probability in a tale, not a reviewer in London but will tell him his theme is the utterly impossible. And, when the thing happens, one may doubt if even then one will get the recognition one deserves.

H. G. Wells

THE WRITING OF ESSAYS

The art of the essayist is so simple, so entirely free from canons of criticism, and withal so delightful, that one must needs wonder why all men are not essayists. Perhaps people do not know how easy it is. Or perhaps beginners are misled. Rightly taught it may be learnt in a brief ten minutes or so, what art there is in it. And all the rest is as easy as wandering among woodlands on a bright morning in the spring.

Then sit you down if you would join us, taking paper, pens, and ink; and mark this, your pen is a matter of vital moment. For every pen writes its own sort of essay, and pencils also after their kind. The ink perhaps may have its influence too, and the paper; but paramount is the pen. This, indeed, is the fundamental secret of essay-writing. Wed any man to his proper pen, and the delights of composition and the birth of an essay are assured. Only many of us wander through the earth and never meet with her—futile and lonely men.

And, of all pens, your quill for essays that are literature. There is a subtle informality, a delightful easiness, perhaps even a faint immorality essentially literary, about the quill. The quill is rich in suggestion and quotation. There are quills that would quote you Montaigne and Horace in the hands of a trades-union delegate. And those quirky, idle noises this pen makes are delightful, and would break your easy fluency with wit. All the classical essayists wrote with a quill, and Addison used the most expensive kind the Government purchased. And the beginning of the inferior essay was the dawn of the cheap steel pen.

The quill nibs they sell to fit into ordinary pen-holders are no true quills at all, lacking dignity, and may even lead you into the New Humour if you trust overmuch to their use. After a proper quill commend me to a stumpy BB pencil; you get less polish and broader effects, but you are still doing good literature. Sometimes the work is close—Mr. George Meredith, for instance, is suspected of a soft pencil—and always it is blunter than quill work and more terse. With a hard pencil no man can write anything but a graceless style—a kind of east wind air it gives—and smile you cannot. So that it is often used for serious articles in the half-crown reviews.

There follows the host of steel pens. That bald, clear, scientific style, all set about with words like "evolution" and "environment," which aims at expressing its meaning with precision and an exemplary economy of words, is done with fine steel nibs—twelve a penny at any stationer's. The J pen to the lady novelist, and the stylograph to the devil—your essayist must not touch the things. So much for the pen. If you cannot write essays easily, that is where the hitch comes in. Get a box of a different kind of pen and begin again, and so on again and again until despair or joy arrests you.

As for a typewriter, you could no more get an essay out of a typewriter than you could play a sonata upon its keys. No essay was ever written with a typewriter yet, nor ever will be. Besides its impossibility, the suggestion implies a brutal disregard of the division of labour by which we live and move and have our being. If the essayist typewrite, the unemployed typewriter, who is commonly a person of superior education and capacity, might take to essays, and where is your living then? One might as reasonably start at once with the Linotype and print one's wit and humour straight away. And taking the invasion of other trades one step further one might, after an attempt to sell one's own newspaper, even get to the pitch of having to read it oneself. No; even essayists must be reasonable. If its mechanical clitter-clatter did not render composition impossible, the typewriter would still be beneath the honour of a literary man.

Then for the paper. The luxurious, expensive, small-sized cream-laid note is best, since it makes your essay choice and compact; and, failing that, ripped envelopes and the backs of bills. Some men love ruled paper, because they can write athwart the lines, and some take the fly-leaves of their friends' books. But whosoever writes on cheap sermon paper full of hairs should write far away from the woman he loves, lest he offend her ears. It is good, however, for a terse, forcible style.

The ink should be glossy black as it leaves your pen, for polished English. Violet inks lead to sham sentiment, and blue-black to vulgarity. Red ink essays are often good, but usually unfit for publication.

This is as much almost as anyone need know to begin essay writing. Given your proper pen and ink, or pencil and paper, you simply sit down and write the thing. The value of an essay is not its matter, but its mood. You must be comfortable, of course; an easy-chair with arm-rests, slippers, and a book to write upon are usually employed, and you must be fed recently, and your body clothed with ease rather than grandeur. For the rest, do not trouble to stick to your subject, or any subject; and take no thought for the editor or the reader, for your essay should be as spontaneous as the lilies of the field.

So long as you do not begin with a definition you may begin anyhow. An abrupt beginning is much admired, after the fashion of the clown's entry through the chemist's window. Then whack at your reader at once, hit him over the head with the sausages, brisk him up with the poker, bundle him into the wheelbarrow, and so carry him away with you before he knows where you are. You can do what you like with a reader then, if you only keep him nicely on the move. So long as you are happy your reader will be so too. But one law must be observed: an essay, like a dog that wishes to please, must have a lively tail, short but as waggish as possible. Like a rocket, an essay goes only with fizzle and sparks at the end of it. And, know, that to stop writing is the secret of writing an essay; the essay that the public loves dies young.

THE PARKES MUSEUM

THE PLACE TO SPEND A HAPPY DAY

By way of jest, my morning daily paper constantly includes in its menu of "To-day" the Parkes Museum, Margaret Street, adding, seductively, "free"; and no doubt many a festive Jonas Chuzzlewit has preened himself for a sight-seeing, and all unaware of the multitudes of Margaret Streets—surely only Charlottes of that ilk are more abundant—has started forth, he and his feminine, to find this Parkes Museum. One may even conceive a rare Bank Holiday thoughtfully put aside for the quest, and spent all vainly in the asking of policemen, and in traversing this vast and tiresome metropolis, from Margaret Street to Margaret Street, the freshness of the morning passing into the dry heat of the day, fatigue spreading from the feet upwards, discussion, difference, denial, "words," and a day of recreation dying at last into a sunset of lurid sulks. Such possibility was too painful to think of, and a philanthropic inquirer has at last by persistent investigation won the secret of the Missing Museum and opened the way to it for all future investigators.

The Margaret Street in question is an apparently derelict thoroughfare, opening into Great Portland Street. Immemorial dust is upon its pavements, and a profound silence broods over its vacant roadway. The blinds of its houses are mostly down, and, where the blackness of some window suggests a dark interior, no face appears to reassure us in our doubt of humanity within. It may be that somewhere in the past the entire population of this street set out on a boating party up the river, and was overset by steam launches, and so never returned, or perchance it has all been locked up for a long term of imprisonment—though the houses seem almost too respectable for that; or the glamour of the Sleeping Beauty is upon it all. Certainly we saw the figure of a porter in an attitude of repose in the little glass lodge in the museum doorway. He *may* have been asleep. But we feared to touch him—and indeed slipped very stealthily by him—lest he should suddenly crumble into dust.

And so to the Museum and its wonders. This Parkes Museum is a kind of armoury of hygiene, a place full of apparatus for being healthy—in brief, a museum of sanitary science. To that large and growing class of people who take no thought of anything but what they eat and what they drink, and wherewithal they should be clothed, it should prove intensely interesting. Apart from the difficulty of approach we cannot understand how it is so neglected by an intelligent public. You can see germicides and a model convict prison, Pentonville cells in miniature, statistical diagrams and drain pipes—if only there was a little more about heredity, it would be exactly the kind of thing that is popular in literature now, as literature goes. And yet excepting ourselves and the sleeping porter—if he was sleeping—and the indistinct and motionless outline, visible through a glass door, of a human body sitting over a book, there was not a suggestion or memory of living humanity about the place.

The exhibits of food are especially remarkable. We cleaned the glass case with our sleeves and peered at the most appetising revelations. There are dozens of little bottles hermetically sealed, containing such curios as a sample of "Bacon Common (Gammon) Uncooked," and then the same cooked—it looked no nicer cooked—Irish sausage, pork sausage, black pudding, Welsh mutton, and all kinds of rare and exquisite feeding. There are ever so many cases of this kind of thing. We saw, for instance, further along, several good specimens of the common oyster shell (*Ostrea edulis*), cockle shells, and whelks, both "almonds" and "whites," and then came breadstuffs. The breadstuffs are particularly impressive, of a grey, scientific aspect, a hard, hoary antiquity. We always knew that stale bread was good for one, but yet the Parkes Museum startled us with the antique pattern it recommended. There was a muffin, too, identified and labelled, but without any Latin name, a captured crumpet, a collection of buns, a dinner-roll, and a something novel to us, called Pumpernickel, that we had rather be without, or rather—for the expression is ambiguous—that we had rather not be without, but altogether remote from. And all these things have been tested by an analyst, with the most painful results. Nitrogen, oxygen, hydrogen, and the like nasty chemical things seem indeed to have occurred in everything he touched. Those sturdy mendicants who go about complaining that they cannot get food should visit this Parkes Museum and see what food is really like, and learn contentment with their lot.

There were no real vegetables, but only the ideals of a firm of seedsmen, made of wax and splendidly coloured, with something of the boldness and vigour of Michael Angelo about the modelling of them. And among other food stuffs were sweetmeats and yellow capers, liver flukes, British wines, and snuff. At last we felt replete with food stuffs, and went on to see the models to illustrate ventilation, and the exhibits of hygienic glazed tiles arranged around a desert lecture-theatre. Hygienic tiles stimulate the eye vigorously rather than relax it by any aesthetic weakness; and the crematory appliances are so attractive as they are, and must have such an added charm of neatness and brightness when alight, that one longs to lose a relative or so forthwith, for the mere pleasure of seeing them in operation.

A winding staircase designed upon hygienic principles, to bump your head at intervals, takes one to a little iron gallery full of the most charming and varied display of cooking-stoves and oil-lamps. Here, also, there are flaunted the resources of civilisation for the Prevention of Accidents, which resources are four, namely, a patent fire-escape, a patent carriage pole, a coal plate, and a dog muzzle. But the labels, though verbose, are scarcely full enough. They do not tell you, for instance, if you wish to prevent cramp while bathing, whether the dog muzzle or the coal plate should be employed, nor do they show how the fire-escape will prevent the explosion of a paraffin lamp. However, this is a detail. We feel assured that no intelligent person will regret a visit to this most interesting and instructive exhibition. It offers you valuable hints how to live, and suggests the best and tidiest way in which you can, when dead, dispose of your body. We feel assured that the public only needs this intimation of its whereabouts to startle the death-like slumbers of Margaret Street with an unaccustomed tumult. And the first to arrive will, no doubt, find legibly and elegantly written in the dust that covers the collection the record of its discovery by Euphemia and me.

H. G. Wells

BLEAK MARCH IN EPPING FOREST

All along the selvage of Epping Forest there was excitement. Before the swallows, before the violets, long before the cuckoo, with only untimely honeysuckle bushes showing a trace of green, two trippers had been seen traversing the district, making their way towards High Beech, and settling awhile near the Forest Hotel. Whether they were belated survivals from last season or exceptionally early hatchings of the coming year, was a question of considerable moment to the natives, and has since engaged the attention of the local Natural History Society. But we know that, as a matter of fact, they were of little omen, being indeed but insignificant people from Hampstead and not true trippers at all, who were curious to see this forest in raw winter.

For some have argued that there is no Epping Forest at all in the winter-time; that it is, in fact, taken up and put away, and that agriculture is pursued there. Others assert that the Forest is shrouded with wrappers, even as a literary man's study is shrouded by dusty women when they clean him out. Others, again, have supposed that it is a delightful place in winter, far more delightful than in summer, but that this is not published, because no writing man hath ever been there in the cold season. And much more of unreal speculation, but nothing which bore upon it the stamp of truth. So these two—and I am one of the two—went down to Epping Forest to see that it was still there, and how it fared in the dismal weather.

The sky was a greasy grey that guttered down to the horizon, and the wind smote damp and chill. There was a white fringe of ice in the cart-wheel ruts, but withal the frost was not so crisp as to prevent a thin and slippery glaze of softened clay upon the road. The decaying triumphal arch outside the station sadly lacked a coat of paint, and was indistinctly regretful of remote royal visits and processions gone for ever. Then we passed shuddering by many vacant booths that had once resounded with the revelry of ninepenny teas and the gingerbeer cork's staccato, and their forms were piled together and their trestles overturned. And the wind ravened, and no human beings were to be seen. So up the hill to the left, and along the road leading by devious windings between the black hedges and through clay wallows to the hilly part round High Beech.

But upon the shoulder of a hill we turned to a gate to scrape off the mud that made our boots unwieldy. At that moment came a threadbare place in the cloudy curtain that was sweeping across the sun, and our shadows showed themselves for an instant to comfort us. The amber patch of sunlight presently slipped from us and travelled down the meadows towards the distant blue of the hills by Waltham Abbey, touching with miraculous healing a landscape erst dead and shrouded in grey. This transitory gleam of light gladdened us mightily at the time, but it made the after-sky seem all the darker.

So through the steep and tortuous village to High Beech, and then leaving the road we wandered in among big trees and down slopes ankle deep with rustling leaves towards Chingford again. Here was pleasanter walking than the thawing clay, but now and then one felt the threat of an infinite oozy softness beneath the stiff frozen leaves. Once again while we were here the drifting haze of the sky became thinner, and the smooth green-grey beech stems and rugged oak trunks were brightly illuminated. But only for a moment, and thereafter the sky became not simply unsympathetic but ominous. And the misery of the wind grew apace.

H. G. Wells

Presently we wandered into that sinister corner of the Forest where the beech trees have grown so closely together that they have had perforce to lift their branches vertically. Divested of leaves, the bare grey limbs of these seem strangely restless. These trees, reaching so eagerly upward, have an odd resemblance to the weird figures of horror in which William Blake delighted—arms, hands, hair, all stretch intensely to the zenith. They seem to be straining away from the spot to which they are rooted. It is a Laocoon grouping, a wordless concentrated struggle for the sunlight, and disagreeably impressive. The trippers longed to talk and were tongue-tied; they looked now and then over their shoulders. They were glad when the eerie influence was passed, though they traversed a morass to get away from it.

Then across an open place, dismal with the dun hulls of lost cows and the clatter of their bells, over a brook full of dead leaves and edged with rusty clay, through a briery thicket that would fain have detained us, and so to a pathway of succulent green, that oozed black under our feet. Here some poor lost wayfarer has blazed his way with rustic seats, now rheumatic and fungus-eaten. And here, too, the wind, which had sought us howling, found us at last, and stung us sharply with a shower of congealing raindrops. This grew to a steady downfall as the open towards Chingford station was approached at last, after devious winding in the Forest. Then, coming upon the edge of the wood and seeing the lone station against the grey sky, we broke into a shout and began running. But it is dismal running on imperfectly frozen clay, in rain and a gusty wind. We slipped and floundered, and one of us wept sore that she should never see her home again. And worse, the only train sleeping in the station was awakened by our cries, and, with an eldritch shriek at the unseasonable presence of trippers, fled incontinently Londonward.

Smeared with clay and dead leaves almost beyond human likeness, we staggered into the derelict station, and found from an outcast porter that perhaps another train might after the lapse of two hours accumulate sufficiently to take us back to

Gospel Oak and a warm world again. So we speered if there were amusements to be got in this place, and he told us "some very nice walks." To refrain from homicide we left the station, and sought a vast red hotel that loomed through the drift on a steep hill, and in the side of this a door that had not been locked. Happily one had been forgotten, and, entering at last, we roused a hibernating waiter, and he exhumed us some of his winter victual. In this way we were presently to some degree comforted, and could play chess until a train had been sent for our relief. And this did at last happen, and towards the hour of dinner we rejoined our anxious friends, and all the evening time we boasted of a pleasant day and urged them to go even as we had gone.

H. G. Wells

THE THEORY OF QUOTATION

The nobler method of quotation is not to quote at all. For why should one repeat good things that are already written? Are not the words in their fittest context in the original? Clearly, then, your new setting cannot be quite so congruous, which is, forthwith, an admission of incongruity. Your quotation is evidently a plug in a leak, an apology for a gap in your own words. But your vulgar author will even go out of his way to make the clothing of his thoughts thus heterogeneous. He counts every stolen scrap he can work in an improvement—a literary caddis worm. Yet would he consider it improvement to put a piece of even the richest of old tapestry or gold embroidery into his new pair of breeks?

The passion for quotation is peculiar to literature. We do not glory to quote our costume, dress in cast-off court robes, or furnish our houses from the marine store. Neither are we proud of alien initials on the domestic silver. We like things new and primarily our own. We have a wholesome instinct against infection, except, it seems, in the matter of ideas. An authorling will deliberately inoculate his copy with the inverted comma bacillus, till the page swims unsteadily, counting the fever a glow of pure literary healthiness. Yet this reproduction, rightly considered, is merely a proof that his appetite for books has run beyond his digestion. Or his industry may be to seek. You expect an omelette, and presently up come the unbroken eggs. A tissue of quotation wisely looked at is indeed but a motley garment, eloquent either of a fool, or an idle knave in a fool's disguise.

Nevertheless at times—the truth must be told—we must quote. As for admitting that we have quoted, that is another matter altogether. But the other man's phrase will lie at times so close in one's mind to the trend of one's thoughts, that, all virtue notwithstanding, they must needs run into the groove of it. There are phrases that lie about in the literary mind like orange peel on a pavement. You are down on them before you know where you are. But does this necessitate acknowledgment to the man, now in Hades, who sucked that orange and strewed the peel in your way? Rather, is it not more becoming to be angry at his careless anticipation?

One may reasonably look at it in this way. What business has a man to think of things right in front of you, poke his head, as it were, into your light? What right has he to set up dams and tunnel out swallow-holes to deflect the current of your thoughts? Surely you may remove these obstructions, if it suits you, and put them where you will. Else all literature will presently be choked up, and the making of books come to an end. One might as well walk ten miles out of one's way because some deaf oaf or other chose to sit upon a necessary stile. Surely Shakespeare or Lamb, or what other source you contemplate, has had the thing long enough? Out of the road with them. Turn and turn about.

And inverted commas are so inhospitable. If you *must* take in another man's offspring, you should surely try to make the poor foundlings feel at home. Away with such uncharitable distinctions between the children of the house and the stranger within your gates. I never see inverted commas but I think of the necessary persecuted mediaeval Jew in yellow gabardine.

At least, never put the name of the author you quote. Think of the feelings of the dead. Don't let the poor spirit take it to heart that its monumental sayings would pass unrecognised without your advertisement. You mean well, perhaps, but it is in the poorest taste. Yet I have seen Patience on a Monument honourably awarded to William Shakespeare, and fenced in by commas from all intercourse with the general text.

H. G. Wells

There is something so extremely dishonest, too, in acknowledging quotations. Possibly the good people who so contrive that such signatures as "Shakespeare," "Homer," or "St. Paul," appear to be written here and there to parts of their inferior work, manage to justify the proceeding in their conscience; but it is uncommonly like hallmarking pewter on the strength of an infinitesimal tinge of silver therein. The point becomes at once clear if we imagine some obscure painter quoting the style of Raphael and fragments of his designs, and acknowledging his indebtedness by appending the master's signature. Blank forgery! And a flood of light was thrown on the matter by a chance remark of one of Euphemia's aunts—she is a great reader of pure fiction—anent a popular novel: "I am sure it must be a nice book," said she, "or she could not get all these people to write the mottoes for the chapters."

No, it is all very well to play with one's conscience. I have known men so sophisticated as to assert that unacknowledged quotation was wrong. But very few really reasonable people will, I think, refuse to agree with me that the only artistic, the only kindly, and the only honest method of quotation is plagiary. If you cannot plagiarise, surely it were better not to quote.

ON THE ART OF STAYING AT THE SEASIDE

A MEDITATION AT EASTBOURNE

To stay at the seaside properly, one should not think. But even in staying at the seaside there are intervals, waking moments when meals come, even if there are no appointed meal-times. Moreover, now and then, one must go to buy tobacco, a matter one can trust to no hireling, lest he get it dry. It cannot be always seaside, even as it cannot be always May, and through the gaps thought creeps in. Going over the cliff and along the parade, and down by the circulating library to the cigar divan, where they sell Parique tobacco, the swinging of one's legs seems to act like a pendulum to the clockwork of one's brain. One meditates all the way, and chiefly on how few people there are who can really—to a critical adept—be said to stay at the seaside.

People seem to think that one can take a ticket to Eastbourne, or Bognor, or Ventnor, and come and stay at the seaside straight away, just as I have known new-hatched under-graduates tell people they were going to play billiards. Thousands and thousands of people think they have stayed at the seaside, and have not, just as thousands of people erroneously imagine they have played whist. For the latter have played not whist, but Bumble-puppy, and the former have only frequented a watering-place for a time. Your true staying at the seaside is an art, demanding not only railway fares but special aptitude, and, moreover, needing culture, like all worthy arts.

H. G. Wells

The most insurmountable difficulty of the beginner is the classical simplicity of the whole thing. To stay at the seaside properly you just spread yourself out on the extreme edge of the land and let the sunlight soak in. Your eyes are fixed upon the horizon. Some have it that your head should be towards the sea, but the best authorities think that this determines blood to that region, and so stimulates thought. This is all the positive instruction; the rest is prohibition. You must not think, and you must not move, neither may you go to sleep. In a few minutes the adept becomes as a god, even as a god that sits upon the lotus leaf. New light and colour come into the sky and sea, and the surges chant his praises. But those who are not of the elect get pins and needles all over them.

It must be freely admitted that staying at the seaside such as this, staying at the seaside in its perfection, is a thing for a select few. You want a broad stretch of beach and all the visible sea to yourself. You cannot be disturbed by even the most idyllic children trying to bury you with sand and suchlike playfulness, nor by boatloads of the democracy rowing athwart your sea and sky. And the absence of friend or wife goes without saying. I notice down here a very considerable quantity of evidently married pairs, and the huge majority of the rest of the visitors run in couples, and are to all appearances engaged. If they are not, I would submit that they ought to be. Probably there is a certain satisfaction in sitting by the sea with the girl you are in love with, or your wife for the matter of that, just as many people undoubtedly find tea with milk and sugar very nice. But the former is no more the way to get the full and perfect pleasure of staying at the seaside than the latter is the way to get the full and perfect flavour of the tea. True staying at the seaside is neither the repetition of old conversations in new surroundings nor the exposure of one's affections to ozone. It is something infinitely higher. It is pure quiescence. It is the experience of a waking inanition savouring of Buddha and the divine.

Now, staying at the seaside is so rarely done well, because of the littleness of man. To do it properly needs many of the elements of greatness. Your common man, while he has life in him, can let neither himself nor the universe alone. He must be asserting himself in some way, even if it is only by flinging pebbles at a stick. That self-forgetfulness which should be a delight is a terror to him. He brings dogs down to the beach to stand between him and the calm of nature, and yelp. He does worse than that.

The meditative man going daily over by the cliff and along the parade, to get his ounce of tobacco, has a sad spectacle of what human beings may be driven to in this way. One sees altogether some hundreds of people there who have heard perhaps that staying at the seaside is good, and who have, anyhow, got thus far towards it, and stopped. They have not the faintest idea how to make themselves happy. The general expression is veiled curiosity. They sit—mostly with their backs to the sea—talking poorly of indifferent topics and watching one another. Most obviously they want hints of what to do with themselves. Behind them is a bank of flowers like those in Battersea Park, and another parallel parade, and beyond are bathing-machines. The pier completely cuts the horizon out of the background. There is a stout lady, in dark blue, bathing. The only glances directed seaward are furtive ones at her. Many seem to be doubting whether this is not what they came down for. Others lean dubiously to the invitations of the boatmen. Others again listen to vocalists and dramatic outcasts who, for ha'pence, render obvious the reason of their professional degradation. It seems eccentric to travel seventy or eighty miles to hear a man without a voice demonstrate that he is unfit to have one, but they do. Anyone curious in these matters need only go to a watering-place to see and, what is worse, to hear for himself. After an excursion train to Eastbourne, upwards of a thousand people have been seen thus heaped together over an oblong space of a mile long by twenty yards wide. Only three miles away there was a towering white cliff overhanging a practically desert beach; and one seagull circled above one solitary, motionless, supine man, really staying at the seaside.

You cannot walk six miles anywhere along the south coast without coming upon one of these heaps of people, called a watering-place. There will be a town of houses behind wherein the people lodge, until, as they think, they have stayed a sufficient time at the sea, and they return, hot, cross, and mystified, to London. The sea front will be bricked or paved for a mile or so, and there will be rows of boats and bathing-machines, and other contrivances to screen off the view of the sea. And, as we have indicated, watering-places and staying by the seaside are incompatible things. The true stayer by the seaside goes into the watering-place because he must; because there is little food, and that uncooked, and no tobacco, between the cliffs and the sea. Having purchased what he needs he flees forth again. What time the whole selvage of England becomes watering-place, there will be no more staying by the seaside at all in the land. But this is a gloomy train of thought that we will not pursue.

There have been those who assert that one end of staying at the seaside is bathing; but it is easy to show that this is not so. Your proper bathing-place is up the river, where the trees bend to the green and brown shadows of the water. There the bath is sweet, fresh out of the sky, or but just filtered through the blue hills of the distant water-shed; and it is set about with flowers. But the sea—the sea has stood there since the beginning of things, and with small prospect of change, says Mr. Kipling, to all eternity. The water in the sea, geologists tell us, has *not been changed for fifty million years!* The same chemist who sets me against all my food with his chemical names speaks of the sea as a weak solution of drowned men. Be that as it may, it leaves the skin harsh with salt, and the hair sticky. Moreover, it is such a promiscuous bathing-place. However, we need scarcely depreciate the sea as a bath, for what need is there of that when the river is clearly better? No one can deny that the river is better. People who bathe in the sea bathe by mistake, because they have come to the side of the sea, and know not how else to use it.

So, too, with the boating. It is hard to imagine how human

beings who have drifted down streams, and watched the brown fish in the shallows, and peered through the tall sedges at the forget-me-nots, and fought with the ropes of the water-lilies, and heard the ripple under the bows, can ever think of going to and fro, pitching spasmodically, in front of a watering-place. And as for fishing—they catch fish at sea, indeed, but it is not fishing at all; neither rods nor flies have they, and there is an end to that matter.

An Eastbourne meditative man returning to where he stays, with his daily ounce of tobacco already afire, sees in the streets what are called by the natives "cherry-bangs," crowded with people, and, further, cabriolets and such vehicles holding parties and families. The good folks are driving away from the sea for the better part of the day, going to Battle and other places inland. The puzzle of what to do with their sea is too much for them, and they are going away for a little to rest their minds. Regarded as a centre of drives one might think an inland place would be preferable to a seaside town, which at best commands but a half-circle. However that may be, the fact remains that one of the chief occupations of your common visitor to the seaside is going away from it. Than this fact there can be nothing more conclusive in support of my argument that ordinary people are absolutely ignorant and incapable of staying by the seaside.

H. G. Wells

CONCERNING CHESS

The passion for playing chess is one of the most unaccountable in the world. It slaps the theory of natural selection in the face. It is the most absorbing of occupations, the least satisfying of desires, an aimless excrescence upon life. It annihilates a man. You have, let us say, a promising politician, a rising artist, that you wish to destroy. Dagger or bomb are archaic, clumsy, and unreliable—but teach him, inoculate him with chess! It is well, perhaps, that the right way of teaching chess is so little known, that consequently in most cases the plot fails in the performance, the dagger turns aside. Else we should all be chess-players—there would be none left to do the business of the world. Our statesmen would sit with pocket boards while the country went to the devil, our army would bury itself in chequered contemplation, our bread-winners would forget their wives in seeking after impossible mates. The whole world would be disorganised. I can fancy this abominable hypnotism so wrought into the constitution of men that the cabmen would go trying to drive their horses in Knights' moves up and down Charing Cross Road. And now and again a suicide would come to hand with the pathetic inscription pinned to his chest: "I checked with my Queen too soon. I cannot bear the thought of it." There is no remorse like the remorse of chess.

Only, happily, as we say, chess is taught the wrong way round. People put out the board before the learner with all the men in battle array, sixteen a side, with six different kinds of moves, and the poor wretch is simply crushed and appalled. A lot of things happen, mostly disagreeable, and then a mate comes looming up through the haze of pieces. So he goes away awestricken but unharmed, secretly believing that all chess-players are humbugs, and that intelligent chess, which is neither chancy nor rote-learned, is beyond the wit of man. But clearly this is an unreasonable method of instruction. Before the beginner can understand the beginning of the game he must surely understand the end; how can he commence playing until he knows what he is playing for? It is like starting athletes on a race, and leaving them to find out where the winning-post is hidden.

Your true teacher of chess, your subtle chess-poisoner, your cunning Comus who changes men to chess-players, begins quite the other way round. He will, let us say, give you King, Queen, and Pawn placed out in careless possible positions. So you master the militant possibilities of Queen and Pawn without perplexing complications. Then King, Queen, and Bishop perhaps; King, Queen, and Knight; and so on. It ensures that you always play a winning game in these happy days of your chess childhood, and taste the one sweet of chess-playing, the delight of having the upper hand of a better player. Then to more complicated positions, and at last back to the formal beginning. You begin to see now to what end the array is made, and understand why one Gambit differeth from another in glory and virtue. And the chess mania of your teacher cleaveth to you thenceforth and for evermore.

It is a curse upon a man. There is no happiness in chess—Mr. St. George Mivart, who can find happiness in the strangest places, would be at a loss to demonstrate it upon the chess-board. The mild delight of a pretty mate is the least unhappy phase of it. But, generally, you find afterwards that you ought to have mated two moves before, or at the time that an unforeseen reply takes your Queen. No chess-player sleeps well. After the painful strategy of the day one fights one's battles over again. You see with more than daylight clearness that it was the Rook you should have moved, and not the Knight. No! it is impossible! No common sinner innocent of chess knows these lower deeps of remorse. Vast desert boards lie for the chess-player beyond the gates of horn. Stalwart Rooks ram headlong at one, Knights hop sidelong, one's Pawns are all tied, and a mate hangs threatening and never descends. And once chess has been begun in the proper way, it is flesh of your flesh, bone of your bone; you are sold, and the bargain is sealed, and the evil spirit hath entered in.

The proper outlet for the craving is the playing of games, and there is a class of men—shadowy, unhappy, unreal-looking men—who gather in coffee-houses, and play with a desire that dieth not, and a fire that is not quenched. These gather in clubs and play Tournaments, such tournaments as he of the Table Round could never have imagined. But there are others who have the vice who live in country places, in remote situations—curates, schoolmasters, rate collectors—who go consumed from day to day and meet no fit companion, and who must needs find some artificial vent for their mental energy. No one has ever calculated how many sound Problems are possible, and no doubt the Psychical Research people would be glad if Professor Karl Pearson would give his mind to the matter. All the possible dispositions of the pieces come to such a vast number, however, that, according to the theory of probability, and allowing a few thousand arrangements each day, the same problem ought never to turn up more than twice in a century or so. As a matter of fact—it is probably due to some flaw in the theory of probability—the same problem has a way of turning up in different publications several times in a month or so. It may be, of course, that, after all, quite "sound" problems are limited in number, and that we keep on inventing and reinventing them; that, if a record were kept, the whole system, up to four or five moves, might be classified, and placed on record in the course of a few score years. Indeed, if we were to eliminate those with conspicuously bad moves, it may be we should find the number of reasonable games was limited enough, and that even our brilliant Lasker is but repeating the inspirations of some long-buried Persian, some mute inglorious Hindoo, dead and forgotten ages since. It may be over every game there watches the forgotten forerunners of the players, and that chess is indeed a dead game, a haunted game, played out centuries ago, even, as beyond all cavil, is the game of draughts.

The artistic temperament, the gay irresponsible cast of mind, does what it can to lighten the gravity of this too intellectual game. To a mortal there is something indescribably horrible in these champions with their four moves an hour—the bare thought of the mental operations of the fifteen minutes gives one a touch of headache. Compulsory quick moving is the thing for gaiety, and that is why, though we revere Steinitz and Lasker, it is Bird we love. His victories glitter, his errors are magnificent. The true sweetness of chess, if it ever can be sweet, is to see a victory snatched, by some happy impertinence, out of the shadow of apparently irrevocable disaster. And talking of cheerfulness reminds me of Lowson's historical game of chess. Lowson said he had been cheerful sometimes— but, drunk! Perish the thought! Challenged, he would have proved it by some petty tests of pronunciation, some Good Templar's shibboleths. He offered to walk along the kerb, to work any problem in mathematics we could devise, finally to play MacBryde at chess. The other gentleman was appointed judge, and after putting the antimacassar over his head ("jush wigsh") immediately went to sleep in a disorderly heap on the sofa. The game was begun very solemnly, so I am told. MacBryde, in describing it to me afterwards, swayed his hands about with the fingers twiddling in a weird kind of way, and said the board went like that. The game was fierce but brief. It was presently discovered that both kings had been taken. Lowson was hard to convince, but this came home to him. "Man," he is reported to have said to MacBryde, "I'm just drunk. There's no doubt in the matter. I'm feeling very ashamed of myself." It was accordingly decided to declare the game drawn. The position, as I found it next morning, is an interesting one. Lowson's Queen was at K Kt 6, his Bishop at Q B 3, he had several Pawns, and his Knight occupied a commanding position at the intersection of four squares. MacBryde had four Pawns, two Rooks, a Queen, a draught, and a small mantel ornament arranged in a rough semicircle athwart the board. I have no doubt chess exquisites will sneer at this position, but in my opinion it is one of the cheerfulest I have ever seen. I remember I admired it very much at the time, in spite of a slight headache, and it is still the only game of chess that I recall with undiluted pleasure. And yet I have played many games.

THE COAL-SCUTTLE

A STUDY IN DOMESTIC AESTHETICS

Euphemia, who loves to have home dainty and delightful, would have no coals if she could dispense with them, much less a coal-scuttle. Indeed, it would seem she would have no fireplace at all, if she had her will. All the summer she is happy, and the fireplace is anything but the place for a fire; the fender has vanished, the fireirons are gone, it is draped and decorated and disguised. So would dear Euphemia drape and disguise the whole iron framework of the world, with that decorative and decent mind of hers, had she but the scope. There are exotic ferns there, spreading their fanlike fronds, and majolica glows and gleams; and fabrics, of which Morris is the actual or spiritual begetter, delight the eye. In summer-time our fireplace is indeed a thing of beauty, but, alas for the solar system! it is not a joy for ever. The sun at last recedes beyond the equinoxes, and the black bogey who has slept awakens again. Euphemia restores the fender kerb and the brazen dogs and the fireirons that will clatter; and then all the winter, whenever she sits before the fire, her trouble is with her. Even when the red glow of the fire lights up her features most becomingly, and flattery is in her ear, every now and then a sidelong glance at her ugly foe shows that the thought of it is in her mind, and that the crumpled roseleaf, if such a phrase may be used for a coal-scuttle, insists on being felt. And she has even been discovered alone, sitting elbows on knees, and chin on her small clenched fist, frowning at it, puzzling how to circumvent the one enemy of her peace.

H. G. Wells

"It" is what Euphemia always calls this utensil, when she can bring herself to give the indescribable an imperfect vent in speech. But commonly the feeling is too deep for words. Her war with this foeman in her household, this coarse rebel in her realm of soft prettiness, is one of those silent ones, those grim struggles without outcry or threat or appeal for quarter that can never end in any compromise, never find a rest in any truce, except the utter defeat of her antagonist. And how she has tried—the happy thoughts, the faint hopes, the new departures and outflanking movements! And even to-day there the thing defies her—a coal-box, with a broad smile that shows its black teeth, thick and squat, filling a snug corner and swaggering in unmanly triumph over the outrage upon her delicacy that it commits.

One of Euphemia's brightest ideas was to burn wood. Logs make even a picturesque pile in a corner—look "uncommon." But there are objections to wood. Wood finely divided burns with gay quirks and jets of flame, and making cheerful crackling noises the while; but its warmth and brightness are as evanescent as love's young dream. And your solid log has a certain irritating inertness. It is an absentee fuel, spending its fire up the chimney, and after its youthful clouds of glory turns but a cheerless side of black and white char towards the room. And, above all, the marital mind is strangely exasperated by the log. Smite it with the poker, and you get but a sullen resonance, a flight of red sparks, a sense of an unconquerable toughness. It is worse than coke. The crisp fracture of coal, the spitting flames suddenly leaping into existence from the shiny new fissures, are altogether wanting. Old-seasoned timber burns indeed most delightfully, but then it is as ugly as coal, and withal very dear. So Euphemia went back to coal again with a sigh. Possibly if Euphemia had been surrounded by the wealth she deserves this trouble would not have arisen. A silent servant, bearing the due dose of fresh fuel, would have come gliding from a mysterious Beneath, restored the waning animation of the grate, and vanished noiselessly again. But this was beyond the range of Euphemia's possibilities. And so we are face to face with this problem of the scuttle again.

At first she would feign there was no such thing as coal. It was too horrible. Only a Zola would admit it. It was the epoch of concealment. The thing purchased was like a little cupboard on four legs; it might have held any convenient trifle; and there was a shelf upon the top and a book of poetry and a piece of crackled Satsuma. You took a little brass handle and pulled it down, and the front of the little cupboard came forward, and there you found your coal. But a dainty little cupboard can no more entertain black coal and inelegant firewood and keep its daintiness than a mind can entertain black thoughts and yet be sweet. This cabinet became demoralised with amazing quickness; it became incontinent with its corruptions, a hinge got twisted, and after a time it acquired the habit of suddenly, and with an unpleasant oscillatory laughing noise, opening of its own accord and proclaiming its horrid secret to Euphemia's best visitors. An air of wickedness, at once precocious and senile, came upon it; it gaped and leered at Euphemia as the partner of her secret with such a familiar air of "I and you" that she could stand it no longer, and this depraved piece of furniture was banished at last from her presence, and relegated to its proper sphere of sham gentility below stairs, where it easily passed itself upon the cook as an exquisite. Euphemia tried to be sensible then, and determined, since she must have coal in her room, to let no false modesty intervene, but to openly proclaim its presence to all the world.

The next thing, therefore, was a cylinder of brass, broadly open above, saying to the world, as it were, "Look! I contain coal." And there were brass tongs like sugar tongs wherewith Euphemia would regale the fire and brighten it up, handing it a lump at a time in the prettiest way. But brass dints. The brazen thing was quiet and respectable enough upstairs, but ever and again it went away to be filled. What happened on these holiday jaunts Euphemia has never ascertained. But a chance blow or worse cause ran a crease athwart the forehead of the thing, and below an almost imperceptible bulging hinted at a future corpulency. And there was complaint of the quantity of polishing it needed, and an increasing difficulty in keeping it bright. And except when it was full to the brim, the lining was unsightly; and this became more so. One day Ithuriel must have visited Euphemia's apartment, and the tarnished brilliancy of the thing stood confessed. For some days there was an interregnum, and a coal-scuttle from downstairs—a black unstable thing on flat foot and with a vast foolish nether lip—did its duty with inelegant faithfulness.

Then Euphemia had a really pretty fancy. She procured one of those big open garden baskets and painted it a pleasant brown, and instead of a garden fork she had a little half horticultural scoop. In this basket she kept her coals, and she tied a pink ribbon on the handle. One might fancy she had been in some dewy garden and had dug a few coals as one might dig up bulbs, and brought them in and put them down. It attracted attention from all her visitors, and set a kind of fashion in the neighbourhood. For a time Euphemia was almost contented. But one day a malignant woman called, and looked at this device through her gilt eye-glasses, while she secretly groped in the dark of her mind for an unpleasant thing to say. Then suddenly she remarked, "Why not put your coal in a bassinette? Or keep it *all* on the floor?" Euphemia's face fell. The thing was undeniably very like a cradle, in the light of this suggestion; the coal certainly did seem a little out of place there; and besides, if there were more than three or four lumps they had a way of tumbling over the edge upon the carpet when the fire was replenished. The tender shoot of Euphemia's satisfaction suddenly withered and died.

So the struggle has gone on. Sometimes it has been a wrought iron tripod with a subtle tendency to upset in certain directions; sometimes a coal-box; once even the noisy old coal-box of japanned tin, making more noise than a Salvation Army service, and strangely decorated with "art" enamels, had a turn. At present Euphemia is enduring a walnut "casket," that since its first week of office has displayed an increasing indisposition to shut. But things cannot stay like this. The worry and anxiety and vexation, Euphemia declares, are making her old before her time. A delicate woman should not be left alone to struggle against brazen monsters. A closed gas stove is happily impossible, but the husband of the household is threatened with one of those beastly sham fires, wherein gas jets flare among firebrick—a mechanical fire without vitality or variety, that never dances nor crackles nor blazes, a monotonous horror, a fire you cannot poke. That is what it will certainly come to if the problem remains unsolved.

H. G. Wells

BAGARROW

Frankly, I detest this Bagarrow. Yet it is quite generally conceded that Bagarrow is a very well-meaning fellow. But the trouble is to understand him. To do that I have been at some pains, and yet I am still a mere theorist. An anthropometric estimate of the man fails to reveal any reason for the distinction of my aversion. He is of passable height, breadth, and density, and, save for a certain complacency of expression, I find no salient objection in his face. He has bluish eyes and a whitish skin, and average-coloured hair—none of them distinctly indictable possessions. It is something in his interior and unseen mechanism, I think, that must be wrong; some internal lesion that finds expression in his acts.

His mental operations, indeed, were at first as inconceivable to me as a crab's or a cockchafer's. That is where all the trouble came in. For that reason alone they fascinated me and aggrieved me. From the conditions of our acquaintance—we were colleagues—I had to study him with some thoroughness, observing him under these circumstances and those. I have, by the bye, sometimes wondered idly how he would react to alcohol—a fluid he avoids. It would, I am sure, be an entirely novel and remarkable kind of Drunk, and I am also certain it would be an offensive one. But I can't imagine it; I have no data. I could as soon evolve from my inner consciousness an intoxicated giraffe. But, as I say, this interesting experience has hitherto been denied me.

Now my theory of Bagarrow is this, that he has a kind of

disease in his ideals, some interruption of nutrition that has left them small and emasculate. He aims, it appears, at a state called "Really Nice" or the "True Gentleman," the outward and visible signs of which are a conspicuous quietness of costume, gloves in all weathers, and a tightly-rolled umbrella. But coupled in some way with this is a queer smack of the propagandist, a kind of dwarfed prophetic passion. That is the particular oddness of him. He displays a timid yet persistent desire to foist this True Gentleman of his upon an unwilling world, to make you Really Nice after his own pattern. I always suspect him of trying to convert me by stealth when I am not looking.

So far as I can see, Bagarrow's conception of this True Gentleman of his is at best a compromise, mainly holiness, but a tinted kind of holiness—goodness in clean cuffs and with something neat in ties. He renounces the flesh and the devil willingly enough, but he wants to keep up a decent appearance. Now a stark saint I can find sympathy for. I respect your prophet unkempt and in a hair shirt denouncing Sin—and mundane affairs in general—with hoarse passion and a fiery hate. I would not go for my holidays with nor make a domestic pet of such a man, but I respect him. But Bagarrow's pose is different. Bagarrow would call that carrying things to extremes. His is an unobtrusive virtue, a compromising dissent, inaggressive aggressions on sin. So I take it. And at times he puts it to you in a drawling argument, a stream of Bagarrowisms, until you have to hurt his feelings—happily he is always getting his feelings hurt—just to stop the flow of him.

"Life," said Bagarrow, in a moment of expansiveness, "is scarcely worth living unless you are doing good to someone." That I take to be the keystone of him. "I want to be a Good Influence upon all the people I meet." I do not think it has ever dawned upon him that he himself is any way short of perfection; and, so far as I can see, the triumph and end of his good influence is cleanliness of cuff, compactness of umbrella, and general assimilation to the Bagarrow ideal.

Hear him upon one's social duties—this living soul in this world of wonders! "In moderation," said Bagarrow, opening out to questions on that matter, "social relaxation is desirable, and I will even go so far as to admit that I think it well to have at hand some pleasant expedient for entertaining people and passing the time. A humorous song or a recitation—provided it is in really good taste—is harmless enough, and sometimes it may even be turned to good account. And everyone should try to master some instrument or other. The flute, perhaps, is as convenient as any; for the fiddle and piano, you know, are difficult and expensive to learn, and require constant practice. A little legerdemain is also a great acquisition for a man. Some may differ from me in that," continued Bagarrow, "but I see no harm in it. There are hundreds of perfectly proper and innocent tricks with coins and bits of paper, and pieces of string, that will make an evening pass most delightfully. One may get quite a little reputation as an entertainer with these things."

"And it is," pursued Bagarrow, quite glowing with liberality, "just a little pharisaical to object to card tricks. There are quantities of really quite clever and mathematical things that one may do with a chosen card, dealing the pack into heaps and counting slowly. Of course it is not for mere pleasuring that I learn these things. It gives anyone with a little tact an opportunity for stopping card-playing. When the pack is brought in, and all the party are intent upon gaming, you may seize your opportunity and take the cards, saying, 'Let me show you a little trick,' or, 'Have you seen Maskelyne's new trick with the cards?' Before anyone can object you are displaying your skill to their astonished eyes, and in their wonder at your cleverness the objectionable game may be indefinitely postponed."

"Yet so set at times is your gambler upon his abominable pursuit," says Bagarrow, "that in practice even this ingenious expedient has been known to fail." He tried it once, it seems, in a race train to Kempton Park, and afterwards he had to buy a new hat. That incident, indeed, gives you the very essence of

Bagarrow in his insidious attacks on evil. I remember that on another occasion he went out of his way to promise a partially intoxicated man a drink; and taking him into a public-house ordered two lemon squashes! Drinks! He liked lemon squash himself and he did not like beer, and he thought he had only to introduce the poor fallen creature to the delights of temperance to ensure his conversion there and then. I think he expected the man to fall upon him, crying "My benefactor!" But he did not say "My benefactor," at anyrate, though he fell upon him, cheerfully enough.

To avoid the appearance of priggishness, which he dreads with some reason, he even went so far as to procure a herb tobacco, which he smokes with the help of frequent sulphur matches. This he recommends to us strongly. "Won't you try it?" he says, with a winning smile. "Just once." And he is the only man I ever met who drinks that facetious fluid, non-alcoholic beer. Once he proposed to wean me upon that from my distinctive vice, which led indeed to our first rupture. "*I* find it delicious," he said in pathetic surprise.

It is one of his most inveterate habits to tell you quietly what he does, or would do under the circumstances. Seeing you at Kipling, he will propound the proposition that "all true literature has a distinct aim." His test of literary merit is "What good does it do you?" He is a great lender of books, especially of Carlyle and Ruskin, which authors for some absolutely inscrutable reason he considers provocative of Bagarrowism, and he goes to the County Council lectures on dairy-work, because it encourages others to improve themselves. But I have said enough to display him, and of Bagarrow at least—as I can well testify—it is easy to have more than enough. Indeed, after whole days with him I have gone home to dream of the realisation of his ideals, a sort of Bagarrow millennium, a world of Bagarrows. All kinds of men—Falstaffs, Don Quixotes, Alan Stewarts, John the Baptists, John Knoxes, Quilps, and Benvenuto Cellinis—all, so to speak, Bagarrowed, all with clean cuffs, tight umbrellas, and temperate ways, passing to and fro in a regenerate earth.

And so he goes on his way through this wonderful universe with his eyes fixed upon two or three secondary things, without the lust or pride of life, without curiosity or adventure, a mere timid missionary of a religion of "Nicer Ways," a quiet setter of a good example. I can assure you this is no exaggeration, but a portrait. It seems to me that the thing must be pathological, that he and this goodness of his have exactly the same claim upon Lombroso, let us say, as the born criminal. He is born good, a congenital good example, a sufferer from atrophy of his original sin. The only hope I can see for Bagarrow, short of murder, is forcible trepanning. He ought to have the seat of his ideals lanced, and all this wash about doing good to people by stealth taken away. It may be he might prove a very decent fellow then—if there was anything left of him, that is.

THE BOOK OF ESSAYS DEDICATORY

I have been bothered about this book this three months. I have written scarcely anything since Llewellyn asked me for it, for when he asked me I had really nothing on hand. I had just published every line I had ever written, at my own expense, with Prigsbys. Yet three months should suffice for one of Llewellyn's books, which consist chiefly of decorous fly-leaves and a dedication or so, and margins. Of course you know Llewellyn's books—the most delightful things in the market: the sweetest covers, with little gilt apples and things carelessly distributed over luminous grey, and bright red initials, and all these delightful fopperies. But it was the very slightness of these bibelots that disorganised me. And perhaps, also, the fact that no one has ever asked me for a book before.

I had no trouble with the title though—"Lichens." I have wondered the thing was never used before. Lichens, variegated, beautiful, though on the most arid foundations, half fungoid, half vernal—the very name for a booklet of modern verse. And that, of course, decided the key of the cover and disposed of three or four pages. A fly-leaf, a leaf with "Lichens" printed fair and beautiful a little to the left of the centre, then a title-page—"Lichens. By H.G. Wells. London: MDCCCXCV. Stephen Llewellyn." Then a restful blank page, and then—the Dedication. It was the dedication stopped me. The title-page, it is true, had some points of difficulty. Should the Christian name be printed in full or not, for instance; but it had none of the fatal fascination of the dedicatory page. I had, so to speak, to look abroad among the ranks of men, and make one of those fretful forgotten millions—immortal. It seemed a congenial task.

I went to work forthwith.

It was only this morning that I realised the magnitude of my accumulations. Ever since then—it was three months ago—I have been elaborating this Dedication. I turned the pile over, idly at first. Presently I became interested in tracing my varying moods, as they had found a record in the heap.

This struck me—

Then again, a little essay in gratitude came to hand—

TO
PROFESSOR AUGUSTUS FLOOD,
Whose Admirable Lectures on
Palaeontology
First turned my Attention to
Literature.

There was a tinge of pleasantry in the latter that pleased me very greatly when I wrote it, and I find immediately overlying it another essay in the same line—

To the Latter-day Reviewer,
These Pearls.

For some days I was smitten with the idea of dedicating my little booklet to one of my numerous personal antagonists, and conveying some subtly devised insult with an air of magnanimity. I thought, for instance, of Blizzard—

SIR JOSEPH BLIZZARD,
The most distinguished, if not the greatest, of contemporary anatomists.

I think it was "X.L.'s" book, *Aut Diabolus aut Nihil*, that set me upon another line. There is, after all, your reader to consider in these matters, your average middle-class person to impress in some way. They say the creature is a snob, and absolutely devoid of any tinge of humour, and I must confess that I more than half believe it. At anyrate, it was that persuasion inspired—

> To the Countess of X.,
> In Memory of Many Happy Days.

I know no Countess of X., as a matter of fact, but if the public is such an ass as to think better of my work for the suspicion, I do not care how soon I incur it. And this again is a pretty utilisation of the waste desert of politics—

> MY DEAR SALISBURY,—Pray accept this unworthy tribute of my affectionate esteem.

There were heaps of others. And looking at those heaps it suddenly came sharp and vivid before my mind that there—there was the book I needed, already written! A blank page, a dedication, a blank page, a dedication, and so on. I saw no reason to change the title. It only remained to select the things, and the book was done. I set to work at once, and in a very little while my bibelot was selected. There were dedications fulsome and fluid, dedications acrid and uncharitable, dedications in verse and dedications in the dead languages: all sorts and conditions of dedications, even the simple "To J.H. Gabbles"—so suggestive of the modest white stones of the village churchyard. Altogether I picked out one hundred and three dedications. At last only one thing remained to complete the book. And that was—the Dedication. You will scarcely credit it, but that worries me still....

I am almost inclined to think that Dedications are going out of fashion.

THROUGH A MICROSCOPE

SOME MORAL REFLECTIONS

This dabbler person has recently disposed of his camera and obtained a microscope—a short, complacent-looking implement it is, of brass—and he goes about everywhere now with little glass bottles in his pocket, ready to jump upon any stray polly-woggle he may find, and hale it home and pry into its affairs. Within his study window are perhaps half a dozen jars and basins full of green scum and choice specimens of black mud in which his victims live. He persists in making me look through this instrument, though I would rather I did not. It seems to me a kind of impropriety even when I do it. He gets innumerable things in a drop of green water, and puts it on a glass slip under the object glass, and, of course, they know nothing of the change in their condition, and go on living just as they did before they were observed. It makes me feel at times like a public moralist, or Peeping Tom of Coventry, or some such creature.

Certainly there are odd things enough in the water. Among others, certain queer green things that are neither plants nor animals. Most of the time they are plants, quiet green threads matted together, but every now and then the inside comes out of one, so to speak, and starts off with a fine red eye and a long flickering tail, to see the world. The dabbler says it's quite a usual thing among the lower plants—*Algae* he calls them, for some reason—to disgorge themselves in this way and go swimming about; but it has quite upset my notions of things.

If the lower plants, why not the higher? It may be my abominable imagination, but since he told me about these— swarm spores I think he called them—I don't feel nearly so safe with my geraniums as I did.

A particularly objectionable thing in these water drops, the dabbler insists upon my spying at is the furious activity of everything you see in them. You look down his wretched tube, and there, bright and yellow with the lamplight in the round field of the microscope, is a perfect riot of living things. Perhaps it's the water he got from Hampstead, and a dozen flat things the shape of shortbreads will be fussing about. They are all quite transparent and colourless, and move about like galleys by means of a lot of minute oars that stick out all over them. Never a moment's rest. And, presently, one sees that even the green plant threads are wriggling across the field. The dabbler tries to moralise on this in the vein of Charles Kingsley, and infer we have much to learn from these ridiculous creatures; but, so far as I can see, it's a direct incentive to sloth to think how low in the scale of creation these things are, in spite of all their fussing. If they had sat about more and thought, they might be fishing the dabbler out of ponds and examining him instead of his examining them. Your energetic people might do worse things than have a meditative half-hour at the microscope. Then there are green things with a red spot and a tail, that creep about like slugs, and are equally transparent. *Euglena viridis* the dabbler calls them, which seems unnecessary information. In fact all the things he shows me are transparent. Even the little one-eyed Crustacea, the size of a needle-point, that discredit the name of Cyclops. You can see their digestion and muscle and nerve, and, in fact, everything. It's at least a blessing we are not the same. Fancy the audible comments of the temperance advocate when you get in the bus! No use pulling yourself together then. "Pretty full!" And "Look," people would say, "his wife gives him cold mutton."

Speaking of the name of Cyclops reminds me that these scientific people have been playing a scurvy trick upon the classics behind our backs. It reminds one of Epistemon's visit to Hades, when he saw Alexander a patcher of clouts and Xerxes a crier of mustard. Aphrodite, the dabbler tells me, is a kind of dirty mud-worm, and much dissected by spectacled pretenders to the London B.Sc.; every candidate, says the syllabus, must be able to dissect, to the examiner's satisfaction, and demonstrate upon Aphrodite, Nereis, Palaemon. Were the gods ever so insulted? Then the snaky Medusa and Pandora, our mother, are jelly-fish; Astraea is still to be found on coral reefs, a poor thing, and much browsed upon by parrot fish; and Doris and Tethys and Cydippe are sea slugs. It's worse than Heine's vision of the gods grown old. They can't be content with the departed gods merely. Evadne is a water flea—they'll make something out of Mrs. Sarah Grand next; and Autolycus, my Autolycus! is a polymorphic worm, whatever subtlety of insult "polymorphic worm" may convey.

However, I wander from the microscope. These shortbread things are fussing about hither and thither across the field, and now and then an amoeba comes crawling into view. These are invertebrate jelly-like things of no particular shape, and they keep on thrusting out a part here, and withdrawing a part there, and changing and advancing just as though they were popular democratic premiers. Then diatoms keep gliding athwart the circle. These diatoms are, to me at least, the most perplexing things in the universe. Imagine a highly ornamental thing in white and brown, the shape of a spectacle case, without any limbs or other visible means of progression, and without any wriggling of the body, or indeed any apparent effort at all, gliding along at a smart pace. That's your diatom. The dabbler really knows nothing of how they do it. He mumbles something about Buetschli and Grenfell. Imagine the thing on a larger scale, Cleopatra's Needle, for instance, travelling on its side up the Thames Embankment, and all unchaperoned, at the rate of four or five miles an hour.

There's another odd thing about these microscope things which redeems, to some extent at least, their singular frankness. To use the decorous phrase of the text-book, "They multiply by fission." Your amoeba or vorticella, as the case may be, splits in two. Then there are two amoebae or vorticellae. In this way the necessity of the family, that middle-class institution so abhorrent to the artistic mind, is avoided. In my friend's drop of ditch-water, as in heaven, there is neither marrying nor giving in marriage. There are no waste parents, which should appeal to the scholastic mind, and the simple protozoon has none of that fitful fever of falling in love, that distressingly tender state that so bothers your mortal man. They go about their business with an enviable singleness of purpose, and when they have eaten and drunk, and attained to the fulness of life, they divide and begin again with renewed zest the pastime of living.

In a sense they are immortal. For we may look at this matter in another light, and say our exuberant protozoon has shed a daughter, and remains. In that case the amoeba I look at may have crawled among the slime of the Silurian seas when the common ancestor of myself and the royal family was an unassuming mud-fish like those in the reptile house in the Zoo. His memoirs would be interesting. The thought gives a solemn tint to one's meditations. If the dabbler wash him off this slide into his tube of water again, this trivial creature may go on feeding and growing and dividing, and presently be thrown away to wider waters, and so escape to live ... after I am dead, after my masterpieces are forgotten, after our Empire has passed away, after the human animal has passed through I know not what vicissitudes. It may be he will still, with the utmost nonchalance, be pushing out his pseudopodia, and ingesting diatoms when the fretful transitory life of humanity has passed altogether from the earth. One may catch him in specimen tubes by the dozen; but still, when one thinks of this, it is impossible to deny him a certain envious, if qualified, respect.

And all the time these creatures are living their vigorous, fussy little lives; in this drop of water they are being watched by a creature of whose presence they do not dream, who can wipe them all out of existence with a stroke of his thumb, and who is withal as finite, and sometimes as fussy and unreasonably energetic, as themselves. He sees them, and they do not see him, because he has senses they do not possess, because he is too incredibly vast and strange to come, save as an overwhelming catastrophe, into their lives. Even so, it may be, the dabbler himself is being curiously observed.... The dabbler is good enough to say that the suggestion is inconceivable. I can imagine a decent amoeba saying the same thing.

THE PLEASURE OF QUARRELLING

Your cultivated man is apt to pity the respectable poor, on the score of their lack of small excitements, and even in the excess of his generous sympathy to go a Toynbee-Halling in their cause. And Sir Walter Besant once wrote a book about Hoxton, saying, among other things, how monotonous life was there. That is your modern fallacy respecting the lower middle class. One might multiply instances. The tenor of the pity is always the same.

"No music," says the cultivated man, "no pictures, no books to read nor leisure to read in. How can they pass their lives?"

The answer is simple enough, as Emily Bronte knew. They quarrel. And an excellent way of passing the time it is; so excellent, indeed, that the pity were better inverted. But we all lack the knowledge of our chiefest needs. In the first place, and mainly, it is hygienic to quarrel, it disengages floods of nervous energy, the pulse quickens, the breathing is accelerated, the digestion improved. Then it sets one's stagnant brains astir and quickens the imagination; it clears the mind of vapours, as thunder clears the air. And, finally, it is a natural function of the body. In his natural state man is always quarrelling—by instinct. Not to quarrel is indeed one of the vices of our civilisation, one of the reasons why we are neurotic and anaemic, and all these things. And, at last, our enfeebled palates have even lost the capacity for enjoying a "jolly good row."

H. G. Wells

There can be no more melancholy sight in the world than that of your young man or young woman suffering from suppressed pugnacity. Up to the end of the school years it was well with them; they had ample scope for this wholesome commerce, the neat give and take of offence. In the family circle, too, there are still plentiful chances of acquiring the taste. Then, suddenly, they must be gentle and considerate, and all the rest of it. A wholesome shindy, so soon as toga and long skirts arrive, is looked upon as positively wrong; even the dear old institution of the "cut" is falling into disrepute. The quarrelling is all forced back into the system, as it were; it poisons the blood. This is why our literature grows sinister and bitter, and our daughters yearn after this and that, write odd books, and ride about on bicycles in remarkable clothes. They have shut down the safety valve, they suffer from the present lamentable increase of gentleness. They must find some outlet, or perish. If they could only put their arms akimbo and tell each other a piece of their minds for a little, in the ancient way, there can be not the slightest doubt that much of this *fin-de-siecle* unwholesomeness would disappear.

Possibly this fashion of gentleness will pass. Yet it has had increasing sway now for some years. An unhealthy generation has arisen—among the more educated class at least—that quarrels little, regards the function as a vice or a nuisance, as the East-ender does a taste for fine art or literature. We seem indeed to be getting altogether out of the way of it. Rare quarrels, no doubt, occur to everyone, but rare quarrelling is no quarrelling at all. Like beer, smoking, sea-bathing, cycling, and the like delights, you cannot judge of quarrelling by the early essay. But to show how good it is—did you ever know a quarrelsome person give up the use? Alcohol you may wean a man from, and Barrie says he gave up the Arcadia Mixture, and De Quincey conquered opium. But once you are set as a quarreller you quarrel and quarrel till you die.

How to quarrel well and often has ever been something of an art, and it becomes more of an art with the general decline of spirit. For it takes two to make a quarrel. Time was when you turned to the handiest human being, and with small care or labour had the comfortable warmth you needed in a minute or so. There was theology, even in the fifties it was ample cause with two out of three you met. Now people will express a lamentable indifference. Then politics again, but a little while ago fat for the fire of any male gathering, is now a topic of mere tepidity. So you are forced to be more subtle, more patient in your quarrelling. You play like a little boy playing cricket with his sisters, with those who do not understand. A fellow-votary is a rare treat. As a rule you have to lure and humour your antagonist like a child. The wooing is as intricate and delicate as any wooing can well be. To quarrel now, indeed, requires an infinity of patience. The good old days of thumb-biting—"Do you bite your thumbs at us, sir?" and so to clash and stab—are gone for ever.

There are certain principles in quarrelling, however, that the true quarreller ever bears in mind, and which, duly observed, do much to facilitate encounters. In the first place, cultivate Distrust. Have always before you that this is a wicked world, full of insidious people, and you never know what villainous encroachments upon you may be hidden under fair-seeming appearances. That is the flavour of it. At the first suspicion, "stick up for your rights," as the vulgar say. And see that you do it suddenly. Smite promptly, and the surprise and sting of your injustice should provoke an excellent reply. And where there is least ground for suspicion, there, remember, is the most. The right hand of fellowship extended towards you is one of the best openings you have. "Not such a fool," is the kind of attitude to assume, and "You don't put upon *me* so easy." Your adversary resents this a little, and, rankling, tries to explain. You find a personal inference in the expostulation.

Next to a wariness respecting your interests is a keen regard for your honour. Have concealed in the privacy of your mind a code of what is due to you. Expand or modify it as occasion offers. Be as it were a collector of what are called "slights," and never let one pass you. Watch your friend in doorways, passages; when he eats by you, when he drinks with you, when he addresses you, when he writes you letters. It will be hard if you cannot catch him smuggling some deadly insult into your presence. Tax him with it. He did not think, forsooth! Tell him no gentleman would do such a thing, thinkingly or not; that you certainly will not stand it again. Say you will show him. He will presently argue or contradict. So to your climax.

Then, again, there is the personal reference. "Meaning me, sir?" Your victim with a blithe heart babbles of this or that. You let him meander here and there, watching him as if you were in ambush. Presently he comes into your spring. "Of course," you say, "I saw what you were driving at just this minute, when you mentioned mustard in salad dressing, but if I am peppery I am not mean. And if I have a thing to say I say it straight out." A good gambit this, and well into him from the start. The particular beauty of this is that you get him apologetic at first, and can score heavily before he rises to the defensive.

Then, finally, there is your abstract cause, once very fruitful indeed, but now sadly gone in decay, except perhaps in specialist society. As an example, let there be one who is gibing genially at some topic or other, at Japanese king-crabs, or the inductive process, or any other topic which cannot possibly affect you one atom. Then is the time to drop all these merely selfish interests, and to champion the cause of truth. Fall upon him in a fine glow of indignation, and bring your contradiction across his face—whack!—so that all the table may hear. Tell him, with his pardon, that the king-crab is no more a crab than you are a jelly-fish, or that Mill has been superseded these ten years. Ask: "How can you say such things?" From thence to his general knowledge is a short flight, and so to his veracity, his reasoning powers, his mere common sense. "Let me tell you, sir," is the special incantation for the storm.

These are the four chief ways of quarrelling, the four gates to this delightful city. For it is delightful, once your 'prentice days are past. In a way it is like a cold bath on a winter's morning, and you glow all day. In a way it is like football, as the nimble aggravation dances to and fro. In a way it is like chess. Indeed, all games of skill are watered quarrels, quarrel and soda, come to see them in a proper light. And without quarrelling you have not fully appreciated your fellow-man. For in the ultimate it is the train and complement of Love, the shadow that rounds off the delight we take in poor humanity. It is the vinegar and pepper of existence, and long after our taste for sweets has vanished it will be the solace of our declining years.

H. G. Wells

THE AMATEUR NATURE-LOVER

It is possible that an education entirely urban is not the best conceivable preparation for descriptive articles upon the country. On the other hand, your professional nature-lover is sometimes a little over-familiar with his subject. He knows the names of all the things, and he does not spare you. Besides, he is subtle. The prominent features are too familiar to him, and he goes into details. What respectable townsman, for instance, knows what "scabiosa" is? It sounds very unpleasant. Then the professional nature-lover assumes that you know trees. No Englishman can tell any tree from any other tree, except a very palpable oak or poplar. So that we may at least, as an experiment, allow a good Londoner to take his unsophisticated eyes out into the sweet country for once, and try his skill at nature-loving, though his botany has been learned over the counter of flower-shops, and his zoology on Saturday afternoons when they have the band in the Gardens. He makes his way, then, over by Epsom Downs towards Sutton, trying to assimilate his mood to the proper flavour of appreciation as he goes, and with a little notebook in the palm of his hand to assist an ill-trained memory. And the burthen of his song is of course the autumn tints.

The masses of trees towards Epsom and Ewell, with the red houses and Elizabethan facades peeping through their interstices, contain, it would seem, every conceivable colour, except perhaps sky-blue; there are brilliant yellow trees, and a kind of tree of the most amazing gamboges green, almost the green of spring come back, and tan-coloured trees, deep brown, red, and deep crimson trees. Here and there the wind has left its mark, and the grey-brown branches and their purple tracery of twigs, with a suggestion of infinite depth behind, show through the rents in the leafy covering. There are deep green trees—the amateur nature-lover fancies they may be yews—with their dense warm foliage arranged in horizontal masses, like the clouds low down in a sunset; and certain other evergreens, one particularly, with a bluish-green covering of upstanding needles, are intensely conspicuous among the flame tints around. On a distant church tower, and nearer, disputing the possession of a gabled red house with a glowing creeper, is some ivy; and never is the perennial green of ivy so delightful as it is now, when all else is alight with the sombre fire of the sunset of the year....

The amateur nature-lover proceeds over the down, appreciating all this as hard as he can appreciate, and anon gazing up at the grey and white cloud shapes melting slowly from this form to that, and showing lakes, and wide expanses, and serene distances of blue between their gaps. And then he looks round him for a zoological item. Underfoot the grass of the down is recovering from the summer drought and growing soft and green again, and plentiful little flattened snail shells lie about, and here and there a late harebell still nods in the breeze. Yonder bolts a rabbit, and then something whizzes by the amateur nature-lover's ear.

They shoot here somewhere, he remembers suddenly; and then looking round, in a palpitating state, is reassured by the spectacle of a lone golfer looming over the brow of the down, and gesticulating black and weird against the sky. The Londoner, with an abrupt affectation of nonchalance, flings himself flat upon his back, and so remains comparatively safe until the golfer has passed. These golfers are strange creatures, rabbit-coloured, except that many are bright red about the middle, and they repel and yet are ever attracted by a devil in the shape of a little white ball, which leads them on through toothed briars, sharp furzes, pricking goss, and thorns; cursing the thing, weeping even, and anon laughing at their own foolish rambling; muttering, heeding no one to the right or left of their career,—demented creatures, as though these balls were their souls, that they ever sought to lose, and ever repented losing. And silent, ever at the heel of each, is a familiar spirit, an eerie human hedgehog, all set about with walking-sticks, a thing like a cylindrical umbrella-stand with a hat and boots and a certain suggestion of leg. And so they pass and are gone.

Rising, the amateur nature-lover finds he has been reclining on a puff-ball. These puff-balls are certainly the most remarkable example of adaptation to circumstances known to English botanists. They grow abundantly on golf grounds, and are exactly like golf-balls in external appearance. They are, however, Pharisees and whited sepulchres, and within they are full of a soft mess of a most unpleasant appearance—the amateur nature-lover has some on him now—which stuff contains the spores. It is a case of what naturalists call "mimicry"—one of nature's countless adaptations. The golf-player smites these things with force, covering himself with ridicule—and spores, and so disseminating this far-sighted and ingenious fungus far and wide about the links.

The amateur nature-lover passes off the down, and towards Banstead village. He is on the watch for characteristic objects of the countryside, and rustling through the leaves beneath a chestnut avenue he comes upon an old boot. It is a very, very old boot, all its blacking washed off by the rain, and two spreading chestnut leaves, yellow they are with blotches of green, with their broad fingers extended, rest upon it, as if they would protect and altogether cover the poor old boot in its last resting-place. It is as if Mother Nature, who lost sight of her product at the tanner's yard, meant to claim her own trampled child again at last, after all its wanderings. So we go on, noting a sardine tin gleaming brightly in the amber sunlight, through a hazel hedge, and presently another old boot. Some hawthorn berries, some hoary clematis we notice—and then another old boot. Altogether, it may be remarked, in this walk the amateur nature-lover saw eleven old boots, most of them dropped in the very sweetest bits of hedge tangle and grassy corner about Banstead.

It is natural to ask, "Whence come all these old boots?" They are, as everyone knows, among the commonest objects in a country walk, so common, indeed, that the professional nature-lover says very little about them. They cannot grow there, they cannot be dropped from above—they are distinctly earth-worn boots. I have inquired of my own domestic people, and caused inquiry to be made in a large number of house-holds, and there does not appear to be any regular custom of taking boots away to remote and picturesque spots to abandon them. Some discarded boots of my own were produced, but they were quite different from the old boot of the outer air. These home-kept old boots were lovely in their way, hoary with mould running into the most exquisite tints of glauco-phane and blue-grey, but it was a different way altogether from that of the wild boot.

A friend says, that these boots are cast away by tramps. People, he states, give your tramp old boots and hats in great profusion, and the modesty of the recipient drives him to these picturesque and secluded spots to effect the necessary change. But no nature-lover has ever observed the tramp or tramp family in the act of changing their clothes, and since there are even reasons to suppose that their garments are not detachable, it seems preferable to leave the wayside boot as a pleasant flavouring of mystery to our ramble. Another point, which also goes to explode this tramp theory, is that these countryside boots *never occur in pairs*, as any observer of natural history can testify....

So our Cockney Jefferies proceeds, presently coming upon a cinder path. They use cinders a lot about Sutton, to make country paths with; it gives you an unexpected surprise the first time it occurs. You drop suddenly out of a sweetly tangled lane into a veritable bit of the Black Country, and go on with loathing in your soul for your fellow-creatures. There is also an abundance of that last product of civilisation, barbed wire. Oh

that I were Gideon! with thorns and briers of the wilderness
would I teach these elders of Sutton! But a truce to dark
thoughts!

We take our last look at the country from the open down
above Sutton. Blue hills beyond blue hills recede into the
remote distance; from Banstead Down one can see into
Oxfordshire. Windsor Castle is in minute blue silhouette to
the left, and to the right and nearer is the Crystal Palace. And
closer, clusters red-roofed Sutton and its tower, then Cheam,
with its white spire, and further is Ewell, set in a variegated
texture of autumn foliage. Water gleams—a silver thread—at
Ewell, and the sinking sun behind us catches a window here
and there, and turns it into an eye of flame. And so to Sutton
station and home to Cockneydom once more.

FROM AN OBSERVATORY

It will be some time yet before the rising of the moon. Looking down from the observatory one can see the pathways across the park dotted out in yellow lamps, each with a fringe of dim green; and further off, hot and bright, is the tracery of the illuminated streets, through which the people go to and fro. Save for an occasional stirring, or a passing voice speaking out of the dimness beneath me, the night is very still. Not a cloud is to be seen in the dark midwinter sky to hide one speck of its broad smears of star dust and its shining constellations.

As the moon rises, heaven will be flooded with blue light, and one after another the stars will be submerged and lost, until only a solitary shining pinnacle of brightness will here and there remain out of the whole host of them. It is curious to think that, were the moon but a little brighter and truly the ruler of the night, rising to its empire with the setting of the sun, we should never dream of the great stellar universe in which our little solar system swims—or know it only as a traveller's tale, a strange thing to be seen at times in the Arctic Circle. Nay, if the earth's atmosphere were some few score miles higher, a night-long twilight would be drawn like an impenetrable veil across the stars. By a mere accident of our existence we see their multitude ever and again, when the curtains of the daylight and moonlight, and of our own narrow pressing necessities, are for a little while drawn back. Then, for an interval, we look, as if out of a window, into the great deep of heaven. So far as physical science goes, there is nothing in the essential conditions of our existence to necessitate that we

H. G. Wells

should have these transitory glimpses of infinite space. We can imagine men just like ourselves without such an outlook. But it happens that we have it.

If we had not this vision, if we had always so much light in the sky that we could not perceive the stars, our lives, so far as we can infer, would be very much as they are now; there would still be the same needs and desires, the same appliances for our safety and satisfaction; this little gaslit world below would scarcely miss the stars now, if they were blotted out for ever. But our science would be different in some respects had we never seen them. We should still have good reason, in Foucault's pendulum experiment, for supposing that the world rotated upon its axis, and that the sun was so far relatively fixed; but we should have no suspicion of the orbital revolution of the world. Instead we should ascribe the seasonal differences to a meridional movement of the sun. Our spectro-scopic astronomy—so far as it refers to the composition of the sun and moon—would stand precisely where it does, but the bulk of our mathematical astronomy would not exist. Our calendar would still be in all essential respects as it is now; our year with the solstices and equinoxes as its cardinal points. The texture of our poetry might conceivably be the poorer without its star spangles; our philosophy, for the want of a nebular hypothesis. These would be the main differences. Yet, to those who indulge in speculative dreaming, how much smaller life would be with a sun and a moon and a blue beyond for the only visible, the only thinkable universe. And it is, we repeat, from the scientific standpoint a mere accident that the present—the daylight—world periodically opens, as it were, and gives us this inspiring glimpse of the remoteness of space.

One may imagine countless meteors and comets streaming through the solar system, unobserved by those who dwelt under such conditions as have just been suggested, or some huge dark body from the outer depths sweeping straight at that little visible universe, and all unsuspected by the inhabitants. One may imagine the scientific people of such a world, calm in their assurance of the permanence of things, incapable almost of conceiving any disturbing cause. One may imagine how an imaginative writer who doubted that permanence would be pooh-poohed. "Cannot we see to the uttermost limits of space?" they might argue, "and is it not altogether blue and void?" Then, as the unseen visitor draws near, begin the most extraordinary perturbations. The two known heavenly bodies suddenly fail from their accustomed routine. The moon, hitherto invariably full, changes towards its last quarter—and then, behold! For the first time the rays of the greater stars visibly pierce the blue canopy of the sky. How suddenly—painfully almost—the minds of thinking men would be enlarged when this rash of the stars appeared.

And what then if *our* heavens were to open? Very thin indeed is the curtain between us and the unknown. There is a fear of the night that is begotten of ignorance and superstition, a nightmare fear, the fear of the impossible; and there is another fear of the night—of the starlit night—that comes with knowledge, when we see in its true proportion this little life of ours with all its phantasmal environment of cities and stores and arsenals, and the habits, prejudices, and promises of men. Down there in the gaslit street such things are real and solid enough, the only real things, perhaps; but not up here, not under the midnight sky. Here for a space, standing silently upon the dim, grey tower of the old observatory, we may clear our minds of instincts and illusions, and look out upon the real.

And now to the eastward the stars are no longer innumerable, and the sky grows wan. Then a faint silvery mist appears above the housetops, and at last in the midst of this there comes a brilliantly shining line—the upper edge of the rising moon.

H. G. Wells

THE MODE IN MONUMENTS

STRAY THOUGHTS IN HIGHGATE CEMETERY

On a sharp, sunlight morning, when the white clouds are drifting swiftly across the luminous blue sky, there is no finer walk about London than the Highgate ridge. One may stay awhile on the Archway looking down upon the innumerable roofs of London stretching southward into the haze, and shining here and there with the reflection of the rising sun, and then wander on along the picturesque road by the college of Saint Aloysius to the new Catholic church, and so through the Waterlow Park to the cemetery. The Waterlow Park is a pleasant place, full of children and aged persons in perambulators during the middle hours of the day, and in the summer evening time a haunt of young lovers; but your early wanderer finds it solitary save for Vertumnus, who, with L.C.C. on the front of him, is putting in crocuses. So we wander down to the little red lodge, whence a sinuous road runs to Hampstead, and presently into the close groves of monuments that whiten the opposite slope.

How tightly these white sepulchres are packed here! How different this congestion of sorrow from the mossy latitude of God's Acre in the country! The dead are crammed together as closely as the living seemed in that bird's-eye view from the Archway. There is no ample shadow of trees, no tangled corners where mother earth may weave flower garlands over her returning children. The monuments positively jostle and elbow each other for frontage upon the footways. And they are so rawly clean and assertive. Most of them are conspicuously new whitened, with freshly-blackened or newly-gilt inscriptions, bare of lichen, moss, or mystery, and altogether so restless that it seems to the meditative man that the struggle for existence, for mere standing room and a show in the world, still rages among the dead. The unstable slope of the hill, with its bristling array of obelisks, crosses and urns, craning one above another, is as directly opposed to the restfulness of the village churchyard with its serene outspreading yews as midday Fleet Street to a Sabbath evening amidst the Sussex hills. This cemetery is, indeed, a veritable tumult of tombs.

Another thing that presently comes painfully home to one is the lack of individuality among all these dead. Not a necessary lack of individuality so much as a deliberate avoidance of it. As one wanders along the steep, narrow pathways one is more and more profoundly impressed by the wholesale flavour of the mourning, the stereotyping of the monuments. The place is too modern for *memento mori* and the hour-glass and the skull. Instead, Slap & Dash, that excellent firm of monumental masons, everywhere crave to be remembered. Truly, the firm of Slap & Dash have much to answer for among these graves, and they do not seem to be ashamed of it.

From one elevated point in this cemetery one can count more than a hundred urns, getting at last weary and confused with the receding multitude. The urn is not dissimilar to the domestic mantel ornament, and always a stony piece of textile fabric is feigned to be thrown over its shoulder. At times it is wreathed in stony flowers. The only variety is in the form. Sometimes your urn is broad and squat, a Silenus among urns; sometimes fragile and high-shouldered, like a slender old maid; here an "out-size" in urns stalwart and strong, and there a dwarf peeping quaintly from its wrapping. The obelisks, too, run through a long scale of size and refinement. But the curious man finds no hidden connection between the carriage of the monument and the character of the dead. Messrs. Slap & Dash apparently take the urn or obelisk that comes readiest to hand. One wonders dimly why mourners have this overwhelming proclivity for Messrs. Slap & Dash and their obelisk and urn.

The reason why the firm produces these articles may be guessed at. They are probably easy to make, and require scarcely any skill. The contemplative man has a dim vision of a grimy shed in a back street, where a human being passes dismally through life the while he chips out an unending succession of these cheap urns and obelisks for his employers' retailing. But the question why numberless people will profane the memory of their departed by these public advertisements of Slap & Dash, and their evil trade, is a more difficult problem. For surely nothing could be more unmeaning or more ungainly than the monumental urn, unless it be the monumental obelisk. The plain cross, by contrast, has the tenderest meaning, and is a simple and fitting monument that no repetition can stale.

The artistic cowardice of the English is perhaps the clue to the mystery. Your Englishman is always afraid to commit himself to criticism without the refuge of a *tu quoque*. He is covered dead, just as he is covered living, with the "correct thing." A respectable stock-in-trade is proffered him by the insinuating shopman, to whom it is our custom to go. He is told this is selling well, or that is much admired. Heaven defend that he should admire on his own account! He orders the stock urn or the stock slab because it is large and sufficiently expensive for his means and sorrow, and because he knows of nothing better. So we mourn as the stonemason decrees, or after the example and pattern of the Smiths next door. But some day it will dawn upon us that a little thought and a search after beauty are far more becoming than an order and a cheque to the nearest advertising tradesman. Or it may be we shall conclude that the anonymous peace of a grassy mould is better than his commercial brutalities, and so there will be an end of him.

One may go from end to end of this cemetery and find scarcely anything beautiful, appropriate, or tender. A lion, ill done, and yet to some degree impressive, lies complacently above a menagerie keeper, and near this is a tomb of some imagination, with reliefs of the life of Christ. In one place a grotesque horse, with a head disproportionately vast, is to be seen. Perhaps among all these monuments the one to Mrs. Blake is the most pleasing. It is a simply and quaintly executed kneeling figure, with a certain quiet and pathetic reverence of pose that is strangely restful against the serried vulgarity around it.

But the tradesman ghoul will not leave us; he follows us up and down, indecently clamouring his name and address, and at last turns our meditation to despair. Certain stock devices become as painful as popular autotypes. There is the lily broken on its stalk; we meet it here on a cross and there on an obelisk, presently on the pedestal of an urn. There is the hand pointing upward, here balanced on the top of an obelisk and there upon a cross. The white-robed angel, free from the remotest shadow of expression, meets us again and again. "All this is mine," says the tradesman ghoul. "Behold the names of me—Slap & Dash here, the Ugliness Company there, and this the work of the Cheap and Elegant Funeral Association. This is where we slew the art of sculpture. These are our trophies that sculpture is no more. All this marble might have been beautiful, all this sorrow might have been expressive, had it not been for us. See, this is our border, No. A 5, and our pedestal No. E, and our second quality urn, along of a nice appropriate text—a pretty combination and a cheap one. Or we can do it you better in border A 3, and pedestal C, and a larger urn or a hangel—"

The meditative man is seized with a dismal horror, and retreats to the gates. Even there a wooden advertisement grins broadly at him in his discomfiture, and shouts a name athwart his route. And so down the winding road to the valley, and then up Parliament Hill towards Hampstead and its breeze-whipped ponds. And the mind of him is full of a dim vision of days that have been, when sculptor and stonemason were one, when the artist put his work in the porch for all the world to see, when people had leisure to think how things should be done and heart to do them well, when there was beauty in the business of life and dignity in death. And he wonders rather hopelessly if people will ever rise up against these damnable tradesmen who ruin our arts, make our lives costly and dismal, and advertise, advertise even on our graves.

HOW I DIED

It is now ten years ago since I received my death warrant. All these ten years I have been, and I am, and shall be, I hope, for years yet, a Doomed Man. It only occurred to me yesterday that I had been dodging—missing rather than dodging—the common enemy for such a space of time. *Then*, I know, I respected him. It seemed he marched upon me, inexorable, irresistible; even at last I felt his grip upon me. I bowed in the shadow. And he passed. Ten years ago, and once since, he and I have been very near. But now he seems to me but a blind man, and we, with all our solemn folly of medicine and hygiene, but players in a game of Blind Man's Buff. The gaunt, familiar hand comes out suddenly, swiftly, this time surely? And it passes close to my shoulder; I hear someone near me cry, and it is over.... Another ream of paper; there is time at least for the Great Book still.

Very close to the tragedy of life is the comedy, brightest upon the very edge of the dark, and I remember now with a queer touch of sympathetic amusement my dear departed self of the middle eighties. How the thing staggered me! I was full of the vast ambition of youth; I was still at the age when death is quite out of sight, when life is still an interminable vista of years; and then suddenly, with a gout of blood upon my knuckle, with a queer familiar taste in my mouth, that cough which had been a bother became a tragedy, and this world that had been so solid grew faint and thin. I saw through it; saw his face near to my own; suddenly found him beside me, when I had been dreaming he was far beyond there, far away over

H. G. Wells

the hills.

My first phase was an immense sorrow for myself. It was a purely selfish emotion. You see I had been saving myself up, denying myself half the pride of life and most of its indulgence, drilling myself like a drill-sergeant, with my eyes on those now unattainable hills. Had I known it was to end so soon, I should have planned everything so differently. I lay in bed mourning my truncated existence. Then presently the sorrow broadened. They were so sorry, so genuinely sorry for me. And they considered me so much now. I had this and that they would never have given me before—the stateliest bedding, the costliest food. I could feel from my bed the suddenly disorganised house, the distressed friends, the new-born solicitude. Insensibly a realisation of enhanced importance came to temper my regrets for my neglected sins. The lost world, that had seemed so brilliant and attractive, dwindled steadily as the days of my illness wore on. I thought more of the world's loss, and less of my own.

Then came the long journey; the princely style of it! the sudden awakening on the part of external humanity, which had hitherto been wont to jostle me, to help itself before me, to turn its back upon me, to my importance. "He has a diseased lung—cannot live long"....

I was going into the dark and I was not afraid—with ostentation. I still regard that, though now with scarcely so much gravity as heretofore, as a very magnificent period in my life. For nearly four months I was dying with immense dignity. Plutarch might have recorded it. I wrote—in touchingly unsteady pencil—to all my intimate friends, and indeed to many other people. I saw the littleness of hate and ambition. I forgave my enemies, and they were subdued and owned to it. How they must regret these admissions! I made many memorable remarks. This lasted, I say, nearly four months.

The medical profession, which had pronounced my death sentence, reiterated it steadily—has, indeed, done so now this ten years. Towards the end of those four months, however, dying lost its freshness for me. I began to detect a certain habitual quality in my service. I had exhausted all my memorable remarks upon the subject, and the strain began to tell upon all of us.

One day in the spring-time I crawled out alone, carefully wrapped, and with a stick, to look once more—perhaps for the last time—on sky and earth, and the first scattered skirmishers of the coming army of flowers. It was a day of soft wind, when the shadows of the clouds go sweeping over the hills. Quite casually I happened upon a girl clambering over a hedge, and her dress had caught in a bramble, and the chat was quite impromptu and most idyllic. I remember she had three or four wood anemones in her hand—"wind stars" she called them, and I thought it a pretty name. And we talked of this and that, with a light in our eyes, as young folks will.

I quite forgot I was a Doomed Man. I surprised myself walking home with a confident stride that jarred with the sudden recollection of my funereal circumstances. For a moment I tried in vain to think what it was had slipped my memory. Then it came, colourless and remote. "Oh! Death.... He's a Bore," I said; "I've done with him," and laughed to think of having done with him.

"And why not so?" said I.

H. G. Wells

ABOUT THE AUTHOR

 **H. G. Wells** (September 21, 1866 – August 13, 1946), born Herbert George Wells, was an English writer best known for such science fiction novels as The Time Machine, The War of the Worlds, The Invisible Man, and The Island of Doctor Moreau. He was a prolific writer of both fiction and non-fiction, and produced works in many different genres, including contemporary novels, history, and social commentary. He was also an outspoken socialist. His later works become increasingly political and didactic, and only his early science fiction novels are widely read today. Wells, along with Hugo Gernsback and Jules Verne, is sometimes referred to as "The Father of Science Fiction".

Herbert George Wells, the fifth and last child of Joseph Wells (a former domestic gardener and at the time shopkeeper and cricketer) and his wife Sarah Neal (a former domestic servant), was born at Atlas House, 47 High Street, Bromley, Kent. The family was of the impoverished lower-middle-class.

A defining incident of young Wells's life is said to be an accident he had in 1874, when he was seven years old, which left him bedridden with a broken leg. To pass the time he started reading, and soon became devoted to the other worlds and lives to which books gave him access; they also stimulated his desire to write.

Choose from Thousands of 1stWorldLibrary Classics By

A. M. Barnard
Ada Leverson
Adolphus William Ward
Aesop
Agatha Christie
Alexander Aaronsohn
Alexander Kielland
Alexandre Dumas
Alfred Gatty
Alfred Ollivant
Alice Duer Miller
Alice Turner Curtis
Alice Dunbar
Allen Chapman
Alleyne Ireland
Ambrose Bierce
Amelia E. Barr
Amory H. Bradford
Andrew Lang
Andrew McFarland Davis
Andy Adams
Angela Brazil
Anna Alice Chapin
Anna Sewell
Annie Besant
Annie Hamilton Donnell
Annie Payson Call
Annie Roe Carr
Annonaymous
Anton Chekhov
Archibald Lee Fletcher
Arnold Bennett
Arthur C. Benson
Arthur Conan Doyle
Arthur M. Winfield
Arthur Ransome
Arthur Schnitzler
Arthur Train
Atticus
B.H. Baden-Powell
B. M. Bower
B. C. Chatterjee
Baroness Emmuska Orczy
Baroness Orczy
Basil King
Bayard Taylor
Ben Macomber
Bertha Muzzy Bower
Bjornstjerne Bjornson

Booth Tarkington
Boyd Cable
Bram Stoker
C. Collodi
C. E. Orr
C. M. Ingleby
Carolyn Wells
Catherine Parr Traill
Charles A. Eastman
Charles Amory Beach
Charles Dickens
Charles Dudley Warner
Charles Farrar Browne
Charles Ives
Charles Kingsley
Charles Klein
Charles Hanson Towne
Charles Lathrop Pack
Charles Romyn Dake
Charles Whibley
Charles Willing Beale
Charlotte M. Braeme
Charlotte M. Yonge
Charlotte Perkins Stetson
Clair W. Hayes
Clarence Day Jr.
Clarence E. Mulford
Clemence Housman
Confucius
Coningsby Dawson
Cornelis DeWitt Wilcox
Cyril Burleigh
D. H. Lawrence
Daniel Defoe
David Garnett
Dinah Craik
Don Carlos Janes
Donald Keyhoe
Dorothy Kilner
Dougan Clark
Douglas Fairbanks
E. Nesbit
E. P. Roe
E. Phillips Oppenheim
E. S. Brooks
Earl Barnes
Edgar Rice Burroughs
Edith Van Dyne
Edith Wharton

Edward Everett Hale
Edward J. O'Biren
Edward S. Ellis
Edwin L. Arnold
Eleanor Atkins
Eleanor Hallowell Abbott
Eliot Gregory
Elizabeth Gaskell
Elizabeth McCracken
Elizabeth Von Arnim
Ellem Key
Emerson Hough
Emilie F. Carlen
Emily Bronte
Emily Dickinson
Enid Bagnold
Enilor Macartney Lane
Erasmus W. Jones
Ernie Howard Pie
Ethel May Dell
Ethel Turner
Ethel Watts Mumford
Eugene Sue
Eugenie Foa
Eugene Wood
Eustace Hale Ball
Evelyn Everett-green
Everard Cotes
F. H. Cheley
F. J. Cross
F. Marion Crawford
Fannie E. Newberry
Federick Austin Ogg
Ferdinand Ossendowski
Fergus Hume
Florence A. Kilpatrick
Fremont B. Deering
Francis Bacon
Francis Darwin
Frances Hodgson Burnett
Frances Parkinson Keyes
Frank Gee Patchin
Frank Harris
Frank Jewett Mather
Frank L. Packard
Frank V. Webster
Frederic Stewart Isham
Frederick Trevor Hill
Frederick Winslow Taylor

Friedrich Kerst
Friedrich Nietzsche
Fyodor Dostoyevsky
G.A. Henty
G.K. Chesterton
Gabrielle E. Jackson
Garrett P. Serviss
Gaston Leroux
George A. Warren
George Ade
Geroge Bernard Shaw
George Cary Eggleston
George Durston
George Ebers
George Eliot
George Gissing
George MacDonald
George Meredith
George Orwell
George Sylvester Viereck
George Tucker
George W. Cable
George Wharton James
Gertrude Atherton
Gordon Casserly
Grace E. King
Grace Gallatin
Grace Greenwood
Grant Allen
Guillermo A. Sherwell
Gulielma Zollinger
Gustav Flaubert
H. A. Cody
H. B. Irving
H.C. Bailey
H. G. Wells
H. H. Munro
H. Irving Hancock
H. R. Naylor
H. Rider Haggard
H. W. C. Davis
Haldeman Julius
Hall Caine
Hamilton Wright Mabie
Hans Christian Andersen
Harold Avery
Harold McGrath
Harriet Beecher Stowe
Harry Castlemon
Harry Coghill
Harry Houidini

Hayden Carruth
Helent Hunt Jackson
Helen Nicolay
Hendrik Conscience
Hendy David Thoreau
Henri Barbusse
Henrik Ibsen
Henry Adams
Henry Ford
Henry Frost
Henry James
Henry Jones Ford
Henry Seton Merriman
Henry W Longfellow
Herbert A. Giles
Herbert Carter
Herbert N. Casson
Herman Hesse
Hildegard G. Frey
Homer
Honore De Balzac
Horace B. Day
Horace Walpole
Horatio Alger Jr.
Howard Pyle
Howard R. Garis
Hugh Lofting
Hugh Walpole
Humphry Ward
Ian Maclaren
Inez Haynes Gillmore
Irving Bacheller
Isabel Cecilia Williams
Isabel Hornibrook
Israel Abrahams
Ivan Turgenev
J.G.Austin
J. Henri Fabre
J. M. Barrie
J. M. Walsh
J. Macdonald Oxley
J. R. Miller
J. S. Fletcher
J. S. Knowles
J. Storer Clouston
J. W. Duffield
Jack London
Jacob Abbott
James Allen
James Andrews
James Baldwin

James Branch Cabell
James DeMille
James Joyce
James Lane Allen
James Lane Allen
James Oliver Curwood
James Oppenheim
James Otis
James R. Driscoll
Jane Abbott
Jane Austen
Jane L. Stewart
Janet Aldridge
Jens Peter Jacobsen
Jerome K. Jerome
Jessie Graham Flower
John Buchan
John Burroughs
John Cournos
John F. Kennedy
John Gay
John Glasworthy
John Habberton
John Joy Bell
John Kendrick Bangs
John Milton
John Philip Sousa
John Taintor Foote
Jonas Lauritz Idemil Lie
Jonathan Swift
Joseph A. Altsheler
Joseph Carey
Joseph Conrad
Joseph E. Badger Jr
Joseph Hergesheimer
Joseph Jacobs
Jules Vernes
Julian Hawthrone
Julie A Lippmann
Justin Huntly McCarthy
Kakuzo Okakura
Karle Wilson Baker
Kate Chopin
Kenneth Grahame
Kenneth McGaffey
Kate Langley Bosher
Kate Langley Bosher
Katherine Cecil Thurston
Katherine Stokes
L. A. Abbot
L. T. Meade

L. Frank Baum
Latta Griswold
Laura Dent Crane
Laura Lee Hope
Laurence Housman
Lawrence Beasley
Leo Tolstoy
Leonid Andreyev
Lewis Carroll
Lewis Sperry Chafer
Lilian Bell
Lloyd Osbourne
Louis Hughes
Louis Joseph Vance
Louis Tracy
Louisa May Alcott
Lucy Fitch Perkins
Lucy Maud Montgomery
Luther Benson
Lydia Miller Middleton
Lyndon Orr
M. Corvus
M. H. Adams
Margaret E. Sangster
Margret Howth
Margaret Vandercook
Margaret W. Hungerford
Margret Penrose
Maria Edgeworth
Maria Thompson Daviess
Mariano Azuela
Marion Polk Angellotti
Mark Overton
Mark Twain
Mary Austin
Mary Catherine Crowley
Mary Cole
Mary Hastings Bradley
Mary Roberts Rinehart
Mary Rowlandson
M. Wollstonecraft Shelley
Maud Lindsay
Max Beerbohm
Myra Kelly
Nathaniel Hawthrone
Nicolo Machiavelli
O. F. Walton
Oscar Wilde

Owen Johnson
P.G. Wodehouse
Paul and Mabel Thorne
Paul G. Tomlinson
Paul Severing
Percy Brebner
Percy Keese Fitzhugh
Peter B. Kyne
Plato
Quincy Allen
R. Derby Holmes
R. L. Stevenson
R. S. Ball
Rabindranath Tagore
Rahul Alvares
Ralph Bonehill
Ralph Henry Barbour
Ralph Victor
Ralph Waldo Emmerson
Rene Descartes
Ray Cummings
Rex Beach
Rex E. Beach
Richard Harding Davis
Richard Jefferies
Richard Le Gallienne
Robert Barr
Robert Frost
Robert Gordon Anderson
Robert L. Drake
Robert Lansing
Robert Lynd
Robert Michael Ballantyne
Robert W. Chambers
Rosa Nouchette Carey
Rudyard Kipling
Saint Augustine
Samuel B. Allison
Samuel Hopkins Adams
Sarah Bernhardt
Sarah C. Hallowell
Selma Lagerlof
Sherwood Anderson
Sigmund Freud
Standish O'Grady
Stanley Weyman
Stella Benson
Stella M. Francis

Stephen Crane
Stewart Edward White
Stijn Streuvels
Swami Abhedananda
Swami Parmananda
T. S. Ackland
T. S. Arthur
The Princess Der Ling
Thomas A. Janvier
Thomas A Kempis
Thomas Anderton
Thomas Bailey Aldrich
Thomas Bulfinch
Thomas De Quincey
Thomas Dixon
Thomas H. Huxley
Thomas Hardy
Thomas More
Thornton W. Burgess
U. S. Grant
Upton Sinclair
Valentine Williams
Various Authors
Vaughan Kester
Victor Appleton
Victor G. Durham
Victoria Cross
Virginia Woolf
Wadsworth Camp
Walter Camp
Walter Scott
Washington Irving
Wilbur Lawton
Wilkie Collins
Willa Cather
Willard F. Baker
William Dean Howells
William le Queux
W. Makepeace Thackeray
William W. Walter
William Shakespeare
Winston Churchill
Yei Theodora Ozaki
Yogi Ramacharaka
Young E. Allison
Zane Grey